In Praise of *Meeting Jesus Christ*

"The door of faith opens to the Person of Jesus Christ. Msgr. Brian Bransfield's latest book, *Meeting Jesus Christ: Meditations on the Word*, invites the reader to be drawn in and meet Jesus so as to love him and make him known and loved."

— Bishop Paul Sirba, Diocese of Duluth

"Msgr. Bransfield shows us that the scenes of the Gospels are not sword-and-sandal dramas. They're our lives. Jesus is walking our streets, and he's healing people who have jobs and emotions and motives that are a lot like yours and mine. 'God loves to hide in the ordinary,' the author tells us as he enlists us in his search party. And our companions as we search are not only Msgr. Bransfield, but also the great cloud of witnesses he invokes, saints like Ambrose, Jerome, Augustine, Bernard, Bonaventure, Thomas More. Msgr. Bransfield's approach is poetic, memorable—and practical, full of time-proven insights as well as fresh life applications."

— Mike Aquilina, Executive Vice-President, St. Paul Center for Biblical Theology, EWTN host, author, dad, mower of lawn and shoveler of snow

"This is not a book to be read; it's to be experienced. Msgr. Bransfield opens up the Scriptures in a way that brings Jesus to life with a tender brilliance that makes it difficult to close the book and end such a profound encounter. Best of all, it's not a 'one-time' read. It's full of insights that can be plumbed and explored over and over again. Rev. Bransfield has given the faithful a true gift in this book!"

— Susan Brinkmann, OCDS, author and staff journalist for Women of Grace.com

DI052064

"C. S. Lewis once said that to write well you don't describe something as good but you must make the reader feel and experience the goodness of the thing itself. This is precisely what Bransfield does. His book *Meeting Jesus Christ* is not just a good analysis of biblical texts, but we actually feel ourselves being drawn into the very dramatic structure of the events themselves. More, Bransfield has the uncanny ability to make Mary, Peter, the healed leper, etc., as real as the people we pass on the street. It is as if we are reliving the biblical events through their hearts and minds, their fears and hopes. Bransfield's use of concrete images, his acute psychological insights, his powerful dramatic sense, and his poetic imagination all combine to enable the reader to recapture the newness and freshness of Christ's ministry.

"Bransfield is a gifted spiritual writer with a powerful dramatic sense and poetic imagination. *Meeting Jesus Christ* is not merely a good analysis of key biblical texts, but the book also opens up for us the dramatic structure of salvation history. Like anamnesis, the past events in the Bible suddenly become alive for us. His insights are like midrashic explanations, which open us up to ever-deepening insights about the Bible and ourselves. Reading this book, precisely because it allows us to grasp spiritual truth at a deep emotional and psychological level, is a healing experience."

— Joseph C. Atkinson, Executive Secretary of the
Catholic Biblical Association

MEETING JESUS CHRIST

Meditations on the Word

Reverend Monsignor J. Brian Bransfield

With a foreword by
Cardinal Francis George, OMI

Pauline
BOOKS & MEDIA

Library of Congress Cataloging-in-Publication Data

Bransfield, J. Brian.
  Meeting Jesus Christ : meditations on the Word / J. Brian Bransfield ; with
a foreword by Cardinal Francis George, OMI.
     pages cm
  Includes bibliographical references.
  ISBN-13: 978-0-8198-4930-4
  ISBN-10: 0-8198-4930-8
  1. Jesus Christ--Biography. 2. Bible. Gospels--Criticism, interpretation, etc.
I. Title.
  BT301.3.B73 2013
  242'.5--dc23

                         2013013404

Cover design by Rosana Usselmann

Cover photo: isockphoto.com

Published by Pauline Books & Media, 50 Saint Pauls Avenue, Boston, MA
02130-3491

Printed in the U.S.A.

www.pauline.org

Pauline Books & Media is the publishing house of the Daughters of Saint
Paul, an international congregation of women religious serving the Church
with the communications media.

1 2 3 4 5 6 7 8 9   17 16 15 14 13

For Martin and Cynthia,
Christian, Daniel, and Andrew

Contents

Foreword xi

Preface xiii

Acknowledgments xvii

INTRODUCTION

The Light of the Word: Praying with Sacred Scripture 1

CHAPTER ONE

The Annunciation 19

CHAPTER TWO

The Nativity of Saint John the Baptist 43

CHAPTER THREE

Christmas: The Nativity of Our Lord 53

CHAPTER FOUR

"Isn't This the Son of Joseph?" 63

CHAPTER FIVE

Casting Out a Demon 73

CHAPTER SIX

Follow Me: The Call of Saint Matthew 79

CHAPTER SEVEN

The Great Catch of Fish 97

CHAPTER EIGHT

The Cleansing of a Leper 103

CHAPTER NINE

The Wedding Feast of Cana 111

CHAPTER TEN

The Pharisee and the Tax Collector 117

CHAPTER ELEVEN

"Zacchaeus, Come Down" 125

CHAPTER TWELVE

The Pool of Bethesda 133

CHAPTER THIRTEEN

Martha and Mary 143

CHAPTER FOURTEEN

The Woman Caught in Adultery 151

CHAPTER FIFTEEN

"Love Your Enemies" 159

CHAPTER SIXTEEN

The Sinful Woman 165

CHAPTER SEVENTEEN

The Unjust Judge 173

CHAPTER EIGHTEEN

The Defenseless God 179

CHAPTER NINETEEN

The Stone Was Moved Away 195

CHAPTER TWENTY

The Sea of Tiberius: The Old Ways
Are Never Far Away 201

CHAPTER TWENTY-ONE

Saint Stephen: The First Martyr 209

AFTERWORD

The God Who Waits 215

Select Bibliography 225

Credits 233

Foreword

William of Saint Thierry, a twelfth-century contemporary of Saint Bernard of Clairvaux, found in prayer the "mirror of faith." Prayer, he wrote, is the context in which faithful but fearful men and women find the courage to remain in wonder before God, immersed in the mysteries that God has revealed to those who love him. Authentic prayer reflects God's initiatives in the world.

In this Year of Faith, Monsignor Brian Bransfield, associate general secretary of the United States Conference of Catholic Bishops, has written a set of exercises designed to help believers today enter into the mysteries of faith through meditative prayer. These introductory remarks can therefore be read, but the book itself must be prayed. It is a workbook.

The exercises in this book will help frame the prayer of those who are neophytes as well as those who are mystics. They draw on Holy Scripture, interpreted according to the analogy of faith, "Bible stories" in their original context and in the context of the Church's liturgical prayer. The interpretations offered are therefore both traditional and original. Poetic reflections open up analogies that bring the text into a lived context. Questions that could distract from prayer become, instead, part of an experience that keeps us close to the living God.

Monsignor Bransfield elicits more than reflection. He invites self-involvement by moving behind the text of Scripture to common elements of human experience that appear in novel ways: silence, speaking, listening, judging, journeying, darkness and light, and the joy that permeates a life shaped by faith and prayer. Prayer reflects and brings to full consciousness what God is doing in our lives.

The unseen partner with whom one enters into these chapters is the Holy Spirit. The Spirit of God waits and listens until prayer makes us ready to welcome him who is already present but often ignored. The Holy Spirit "groans" in us, as Saint Paul says so forcefully, when we surrender ourselves to prayer. The Paraclete speaks for us, as advocate when we are in the world's courts, or as comforter when we are trembling before the majesty of God. "Receive the Holy Spirit," (Jn 20:22) the risen Christ tells his disciples. Prayer creates a haven in us for God to act, a home where we can live as sons and daughters of a God who wants us to be holy and who listens for signs of our readiness as much as we watch for signs of his presence.

It's been said that the Bible is as much anthropology for God as it is theology for us. Monsignor Bransfield writes in the interstice between God's will and our desires. Prayer purifies our hearts until all that we desire is what God wants for us. Since God wants for us infinitely more than we can want for ourselves, prayer is never finished. There is always more. Christ is always more.

This book guides us into ways still unknown, even to its author. For that reason, in particular, we owe him a debt of gratitude for his work.

CARDINAL FRANCIS GEORGE, OMI

Archbishop of Chicago

Feast of the Holy Name of Jesus, January 3, 2013

Preface

This book is about Jesus Christ. It is not about tasks or techniques; it is not a "how-to" book. It has no "steps." In fact, it *takes a step back*. Moreover, one does not need a degree in theology to understand the message of these pages. One only needs the desire to meet Jesus, because this book points to a personal encounter with Jesus Christ, the Son of the living God, in his Church. Whenever we approach Jesus, he always does more than we do; however much we are searching for him, he searches for us all the more. When we take one step back, God takes three steps forward. Taking such a step back is to risk letting go of fear so as to look at God.

This book is about allowing the act of faith and the new life of grace to shed new and deeper light on our life's journey and our daily decisions. This book is not meant to *become another task*. It will accomplish its purpose if through its pages the reader focuses on Jesus, is drawn even for a brief moment into meditation, or thinking about Jesus, and *for a time forgets time and remembers God*. In fact, the reader who turns these pages might even forget time in the encounter with Jesus so that he or she ends up being late for an otherwise incidental appointment. If that happens, the book will have accomplished its initial purpose.

When we read the Bible or hear the words of Scripture proclaimed at Mass, we are not simply readers or listeners. The Second Vatican Council reminds us that Jesus Christ is present in his word; that "it is he himself who speaks when the holy Scriptures are read in the Church."[1] As we read and listen, *something* more than reading and listening happens: We are *actors* in the drama itself. We are meant to be "drawn in," not simply to "read over." This is because we *meet Jesus* in Sacred Scripture, which is the revealed word of God read with and in his Church. As we listen in faith we hear, in the Church, the one message of Christ, his one plan of salvation and sanctification. The authentic proclamation of the word of God takes place only on the foundation of the apostles in the context of apostolic succession.[2] This is not a private or elitist knowledge meant only for a privileged and select few.[3] It is the universal saving truth for all to hear.

This book you are now holding is a guide to meeting Jesus Christ through meditation on the revealed word. It consists of twenty-one chapters. The Introduction explains the way in which the word of God is a light for us. Each of the chapters takes up a different scriptural account, helping us to step into a meditation on a mystery from the life of Jesus. The various chapters provide meditations on such familiar events as the Annunciation, the Nativity of Saint John the Baptist, the Nativity of Our Lord, Jesus preaching in Nazareth, his casting out of a demon, the call of Saint Matthew, the great catch of

---

1. Vatican Council II, *Sacrosanctum Concilium*, 7; see also Pope Benedict XVI, *Verbum Domini*, 72.

2. See International Theological Commission, *Theology Today: Perspectives, Principles and Criteria* (Rome: Libreria Editrice Vaticana, 2012), 10.

3. See Bertrand de Margerie, SJ, *The Christian Trinity in History: Studies in Historical Theology* (Still River, MA: Saint Bede's Press, 1982), 64.

fish, the cleansing of the leper, the wedding feast of Cana, and many more.

The book has a threefold purpose. The first goal is to open up the Scripture passage so that readers hear something new in these familiar passages, something they have not previously heard. The second goal builds on the first. Even though this is not a "how-to" book, once readers have read these meditations, on their own they can move on to meditate on other passages they may hear or read. Once familiar with the style of meditation presented here, readers may find a fresh approach to reading Scripture. The third goal is that this book itself will be left behind as readers put it down and pick up the Scriptures themselves. Therefore, the third and ultimate purpose of this book is to get out of the way and to *give way* to Christ. Across the spectrum of meditations presented here, the trajectory always remains the encounter with Christ in his mystery.

The book allows for a flexible approach. Readers can begin with page one and go straight through as one chapter flows into the next. Or they can parachute in and begin anywhere, since each chapter is written to stand on its own, and because God is everywhere in his word.

As we begin, and no matter *how many times* we begin again, we are never alone. The Holy Spirit is with us, within us, and within the text we read. The Holy Spirit overcomes our complexity, disables our fear, and introduces us to Jesus.

If we truly want to know the God within, one person above all others is eager to introduce us: Mary. In every age it is she who takes man by the hand and leads him into the very heart of her Divine Son. There she shushes us, telling us to be still in prayer, to listen, and to "Do whatever he tells you" (Jn 2:5).

Acknowledgments

One of my earliest memories as a young child is sitting with my mother and my father as they would read me stories from my picture Bible. After they read the words they would describe the biblical scene presented in the pictures. They'd point to the sky, the persons, the surrounding features of the biblical scene, and continue to explain to me the great action of God.

Those images still remain in my mind today. Those moments were my first experience of contemplation. The pages that follow are, in a real sense, an extension of those profound early moments. And so, my first word of gratitude on the publication of this book goes to my mother and father, now gone to God, for the faith they patiently and devotedly handed on to me and to my brother, Paul, and my sisters Margaret Anne, Mary Jane, and Paula. How blessed my family is to see that faith handed on now to my grandnephews Stephen, David, and Connor, and my grandniece, Katherine.

I am very thankful to all who have supported me in writing this text. A word of most sincere thanks goes to my archbishop, the Most Reverend Charles J. Chaput, OFM Cap, archbishop of Philadelphia, for the inspiration and confidence he inspires through his steadfast example and focused faithful leadership. I am humbled by the very thoughtful foreword to this work offered by His Eminence Cardinal Francis George, OMI, archbishop of Chicago. The Cardinal's dedication to the Church is a genuine inspiration to so many.

The expert staff of the United States Conference of Catholic Bishops, with whom I am privileged to serve, never ceases to be a source of brilliant insight and support. I am grateful to my brother priests who serve at the Conference, as well as my colleagues in the general secretariat, and most especially to Reverend Monsignor Ronny Jenkins, general secretary, for his unfailing dedication to specialized scholarship, professional excellence in leadership, and his friendship. Likewise, I am grateful to Dr. Andrew Lichtenwalner and Dr. Peter Murphy.

The highly skilled efforts of the Daughters of Saint Paul were evident at every stage of the preparation of the manuscript for publication. I am appreciative of the hard work of Sisters Sean Mayer, FSP, and Marianne Lorraine Trouvé, FSP, Ms. Holly Kalinski, Ms. Vanessa Reese, Ms. Brittany Schlorff, and Mr. Brad McCraken.

A strong word of thanks is joyfully extended to my brother priests, the Reverends John Pidgeon, James Olson, Michael Gerlach, Eric Gruber, and Stephen Dougherty (who sadly passed away before the publication of this book) for their fraternal support. Finally, I am grateful to Brian and Joan Gail and to Martin and Cynthia Lutschaunig and their sons, Christian, Daniel, and Andrew, for their friendship.

The Light of the Word: Praying with Sacred Scripture

The purpose of life is to track down God. The task *within* all of our other important daily tasks is ultimately *to track down God* in and through the moment before us. Many actions make up our daily life. We have to stop at the supermarket, pick up the dry cleaning, fill the car with gas. Our ordinary daily tasks may seem random, unconnected, and even repetitive. But God loves to hide in the ordinary. The noted thirteenth-century Carthusian Hugh of Balma taught that God, in a way that is faster than our human thinking, makes countless varied attempts every day—hundreds or thousands of times, day or night—to draw the human soul to himself, train us in his ways, and renew us according to his will.[1]

---

1. See Hugh of Balma, "The Roads to Zion Mourn" in *Carthusian Spirituality: The Writings of Hugh of Balma and Guigo de Ponte*. The Classics of Western Spirituality Series (Mahwah, NJ: Paulist Press, 1997), 71. See also a homily by an anonymous writer of the fourth century (Hom. 18, 7–11: PG 34, 639–642) for the second reading from the Office of Readings for Friday of the Fourth Week in Ordinary Time.

This means that God is always near us. Saint Alphonsus Liguori tells us that when we sleep at night God is closer to us than the very pillow on which we lay our heads, and that even during the night God does not want our conversation with him to pause.[2] The psalmist confirms this: "If you try my heart, if you visit me by night, if you test me, you will find no wickedness in me . . ." (Ps 17:3) and "By day may the Lord send his mercy, and by night may his righteousness be with me!" (Ps 42:8 NAB). The *Catechism of the Catholic Church* notes that God always takes the initiative in calling us to prayer, and he is tireless in doing so.[3]

The interior goal of every action and of daily life itself is to discover in each hour and in each moment *the One who is Life Itself.* Only in this discovery do we reach genuine reality. Without God at the center, everything else detours into worry, confusion, disorder, and ultimately, sin. The baptized Christian, with original sin forgiven, has already met Jesus Christ in his death and resurrection and has become a member of the Church. The baptized Christian has received the Holy Spirit and is strengthened to live the life of grace and virtue. As Catholics, our life is centered on Christ in the Holy Eucharist, whom we adore and receive during Sunday Mass, as well as the forgiveness of sins through regular reception of the Sacrament of Penance. All the daily moments of our week point to and lead from the Sunday Mass celebration. From this center, in and through the Church, we can recognize God at the center of all

---

2. Saint Alphonsus de Liguori, "Conversing with God as a Friend" in *Alphonsus de Liguori: Selected Writings.* The Classics of Western Spirituality Series (Mahwah, NJ: Paulist Press, 1999), 277. See also Adrienne von Speyr, *Mark: Meditations on the Gospel of Mark* (San Francisco: Ignatius Press, 2012), 222.

3. *CCC*, no. 2567, 2575; see also Paul Murray, OP, *The New Wine of Dominican Spirituality: A Drink Called Happiness* (London: Burns and Oates, 2011), 21.

we do through the week. Sacred Scripture gives us the prime coordinates by which we pick up his path.

Praying with Sacred Scripture

In Sacred Scripture the triune God freely discloses beyond all expectation the mystery of God's own life and loving plan for our salvation. Through the words of Scripture we are touched and shaped by all that God has revealed and offered. Upon hearing his word we respond with an act of living faith, and take to ourselves the complete truth of Jesus Christ revealed in and through the authentic teaching of the Church. As Pope Benedict XVI has emphasized, the life of the Church is the primary setting for scriptural interpretation.[4] Through the working of the Holy Spirit and the guidance of the magisterium, the Church hands on to every new generation all that has been revealed in Christ.[5]

Opening the Scriptures is not like opening the pages of the recent best-selling novel, popular magazine, or even the dictionary. As we open the Scriptures and begin to read, something begins to happen. The psalmist proclaims: "The unfolding of your words gives light; it imparts understanding to the simple" (Ps 119:130). Pope Benedict speaks about the word of God as a true light.[6] A light comes forth from the Scriptures. This light does not come from a bulb or candle, nor does it depend on electricity or wax. The light of the word of God is brighter than all other kinds of light.

The light of the word of God is so bright, in fact, that only the heart can detect and see its brilliance. When the heart sees

---

4. See Pope Benedict XVI, *Verbum Domini*, 29.

5. Ibid., 18.

6. Ibid., 12.

this light, it immediately wants to tell the mind. But the mind is often preoccupied and busy. Sin and the ways of the world get in the way. But the heart hopes; it never ceases to call to the mind. With the urgency and insistency of a child, the heart continues to show to the mind the most ordinary things: a leaf, a rock, a sunset or sunrise, or a book, a sentence, phrase, or word—especially the word, the divinely revealed word of God. And the heart wants the mind to see and hear what the heart sees and hears. The Holy Spirit tirelessly assists the heart to see that all things point to an awareness of the presence of God— that all things lead to the worship of Christ in the Holy Eucharist and the forgiveness of sins in the Sacrament of Penance, love of neighbor, and the life of virtue.

In a particular way, the Holy Spirit takes the Sacred Scripture, the inspired word of God, and wants to announce its message to our heart and mind. Perhaps we studied it in grade school, high school, or college. Whenever we see the Bible, we sense a gentle tug at our heart. We feel the invitation to open it, to read it, to spend more time in its depths. We hunger for an authentic prayer life. The Holy Spirit invites us to this profound dialogue.[7] As he seeks to awaken us, the Holy Spirit knows how to wait a long, long time.

If we take the Holy Spirit up on this invitation and begin to read the Sacred Scriptures, we will see a glimmer of light—the light of Jesus Christ. Cardinal Henri de Lubac, SJ, renowned patristic scholar, tells us that Christ is *the fact* that dominates all history, and is the source of all light in which all else culminates.[8] This is one reason why prayer is necessary for us: in

---

7. See Congregation for the Doctrine of the Faith, *Letter to the Bishops of the Catholic Church on Some Aspects of Christian Meditation* (1989), 5.

8. See Henri de Lubac, *Scripture in the Tradition* (New York: Herder and Herder, 1968), 164.

prayer we speak with God, and he speaks with us (see Mt 7:7; Lk 11:9ff.; Mt 26:41). In prayer God leads us away from evil and fosters our inclination to do good. Prayer is not a time to concentrate on ourselves but on Jesus Christ and the inexhaustible promise of his love. Prayer is not a time for us to seek some type of psychological or emotional experience but the mystery of Jesus Christ.[9] While all things are possible for God, we do not focus on exceptional states or unusual phenomenon that at times may accompany prayer but on meditation, which makes one receptive to internalizing the life of virtue.[10]

Prayer can take many forms. The Mass is the preeminent prayer, followed by the Divine Office, also known as the Liturgy of the Hours.[11] This prayer sanctifies the day. It leads from and returns to the Mass. Saint John Cassian, the fourth-century theologian and monk who had tremendous influence on Saint Benedict, noted that the psalm invocation that begins the hours, "O God, come to my assistance. O Lord make haste to help me" (Ps 70:1), is of absolute necessity for the one who would remain aware of God's presence.[12] This verse is so significant and time-tested that one thousand years later the anonymous English author of *The Cloud of Unknowing* references the Desert Fathers' use of it.[13] Saint Alphonsus Liguori, writing in Italy in

---

9. See Congregation for the Doctrine of the Faith, *Christian Meditation,* 9.

10. See Jean-Pierre Torrell, OP, *Christ and Spirituality in Saint Thomas Aquinas* (Washington, DC: The Catholic University of America Press, 2011), 2.

11. See A. G. Martimort, et al., "The Liturgy and Time" in *The Church at Prayer,* vol. IV (Collegeville, MN: The Liturgical Press, 1986), 151ff.

12. See *CCC,* no. 2785. See also John Cassian, *The Conferences,* trans. Boniface Ramsey, OP, The Classics of Western Spirituality Series (Mahwah, NJ: Paulist Press, 1997), X.X.2; 379; see also Gertrude Gillette, OSB, *Four Faces of Anger: Seneca, Evagrius Ponticus, Cassian, and Augustine* (Lanham, MD: University Press of America, 2010), xiii.

13. See *The Cloud of Unknowing,* trans. James Walsh, SJ, in The Classics of Western Spirituality Series (Mahwah, NJ: Paulist Press, 1981), 134.

the eighteenth century, also notes that this verse was the crucial prayer of the Desert Fathers.[14]

Marian prayers, such as the Holy Rosary, the Novena to Our Lady of the Miraculous Medal, and the Angelus, are prayers central to the Christian spiritual life. Adrienne von Speyr reminds us that even those prayers we know very well and whose words never change are always heard by God in a new way, as if for the first time.[15] The *Catechism of the Catholic Church* teaches, "The invocation of the holy name of Jesus is the simplest way of praying always."[16] In addition, we can practice the momentary prayer of calling God to mind with or without words.[17]

Likewise, the *Catechism* explains, "Every time we begin to pray to Jesus it is the Holy Spirit who draws us on the way of prayer by his prevenient grace."[18] It further teaches that the "Spirit is offered us at all times, in the events of each day, to make prayer spring up from us . . . Prayer in the events of *each day* and each moment is one of the secrets of the kingdom . . ."[19] The *Catechism* urges us to call on the Holy Spirit each day, in particular as we begin and end every important action.[20]

Another very effective form of prayer is devotion to one's patron saint. Meditation on the lives of various other saints, as

---

14. See also Saint Alphonsus de Liguori, "The Practice of the Love of Jesus" in *Alphonsus de Liguori: Selected Writings*, 150.

15. See Adrienne von Speyr, *The World of Prayer* (San Francisco: Ignatius Press, 1985), 179, 248.

16. *CCC*, no. 2668.

17. See Simon Tugwell, OP, *Prayer: Living with God* (Springfield, IL: Templegate, 1975), 14. See also Linette Martin, *Practical Praying* (Grand Rapids, MI: Wm. B. Eerdmans Publishing Company, 1997), 11.

18. *CCC*, no. 2670. See also Hans Urs von Balthasar, *Theologic III: The Spirit of Truth* (San Francisco: Ignatius Press, 2005), 272.

19. *CCC*, nos. 2659–2660.

20. *CCC*, no. 2670.

well, draws us to prayer. Pope Benedict XVI compares the saint to a ray of light that comes forth from the word of God.[21] Saint Ambrose says that prayer is a cry of the heart.[22] The author of the *Cloud of Unknowing* also wrote a little-known book entitled *The Assessment of Inward Stirrings*. In this work, the author notes that even the smallest reverent stirring of lasting love, along with awareness of God, can lead us deeper into his mystery.[23] We pray not in order to change the will of God, but so that his will might truly be fulfilled.[24] As we pray we grow in intimacy with God, and this closeness gives us the strength to live even in situations that do not turn out as we would have them. The word of Christ is a light that interiorizes his life within us.

Sin

As we know all too well, sin is the enemy of the new life of grace and leads us away from prayer. Sin is the disobedient choice by which man, as a creature, insists on his self-sufficient way, rebelliously refuses to do the will of God, and rejects God. Sin, the refusal of divine love, offends God. Venial sin is disobedience to God that harms the life of grace within us by weakening it, though it does not completely destroy it. Mortal sin is the free and deliberate choice of the will, made with sufficient reflection, to oppose God in a serious matter. By this we drive the life of sanctifying grace from our hearts and are deprived of friendship with God. Sin is incompatible with holiness.

---

21. See Pope Benedict XVI, *Verbum Domini*, 48.

22. See Saint Ambrose, *Exposition* on Psalm 118.

23. "The Assessment of Inner Stirrings" in *The Pursuit of Wisdom and Other Works by the Author of the Cloud of Unknowing*. The Classics of Western Spirituality Series (Mahwah, NJ: Paulist Press, 1988), 142.

24. See Jean-Pierre Torrell, OP, *Christ and Spirituality in Saint Thomas Aquinas*, 70–71.

Even after we sin, God, through the gift of grace, still seeks us out and stirs us to return to him, in particular through the Sacrament of Penance. God longs to share the gift of mercy and forgiveness with us. It is we who are so often stubborn and delay our return to him and his Church. It is as if, even when we realize we have sinned, our ego kicks in with an extra dose of pride and conjures a false industrious spirit that lures us into the notion, "I got myself into sin, I will get myself out of it." The ego can also be subtle, suggesting to us that we know God so well that we do not have to follow the teachings of the Church, that our spiritual life is just a private matter between God and us. These, however, are common tricks of the Evil One, disguised with a misleading focus back upon ourselves rather than on Christ and his Church. This deceptive detour is actually engineered to draw us further into complacency, and thus toward sin, by means of the illusion of self-sufficiency. But even here, God reaches out all the more to call us to confess our sins and receive forgiveness and mercy.

Distractions

In addition to the deception of sin, we face other obstacles to prayer, such as distractions, routine, and boredom. Our human frailty is never far away. The temptations and illusions of the world continuously seek entry into our heart. The world always goes to extremes: It either induces us to crave more and more things, or to slip into a kind of sluggish and self-centered inertia, moored by old memories that never seem to heal. But Jesus Christ, the Word made flesh, is the sustaining center of all prayer. He is the fount of all grace and the unshakeable source of all virtue. Even our distractions cannot elude him.

We are to pray our distractions *into* the prayer we offer. Saint Teresa of Avila refreshingly points out that God values very highly even the brief moments we spend in prayer, moments when we may feel lukewarm or less than excited.[25] The Holy Spirit dwells in us and works undisturbed with divine love in the deep places of our soul. He seeks all the more to inspire us, even in moments of distraction and dryness in prayer. He helps to dispose us so that we are ready and docile at his prompting to turn our minds and hearts to Christ.

Throughout the Gospels we see the light of Jesus made visible with sharp focus and distinct clarity. The Holy Spirit longs to cast this light deep into our hearts, and he is, in fact, already doing so. He patiently casts his light by means of the Church's ministry. The Church makes known the mysteries of Divine Revelation and points to the beauty of natural reason to find the signs that point to God. Spirituality is not a fad or an option. Spirituality is not first an individual choice. It is not me simply finding the "right" spirituality for me. It is, rather, me *being found* by God. Spirituality is our total response in faith, sustained by grace, nurtured through love, and strengthened by the action of the Holy Spirit, to all that God has revealed in Christ made known in and through the Church.[26]

The world will attempt to prevent this meeting. The devil seeks to lull us away from God into a lethargic and inimical kind of *sub*-consciousness. Authentic prayer wakes us up from this delirium. The world attempts to fill our thoughts with anything but God. Some people place more faith in the sales pitch of commercials than they do in the age-old truth of God's love and his word. Simply listen to the tag line of the dozens, if not

---

25. See Saint Teresa of Avila, *The Interior Castle* in *The Collected Works of Saint Teresa of Avila,* trans. Otilio Rodriguez, OCD, and Kieran Kavanaugh, OCD (Washington DC: ICS Publications, 1980), II.1.3; 298.

26. See Prosper Grech, *An Outline of New Testament Spirituality* (Grand Rapids, MI: Wm. B. Eerdmans Publishing Company, 2011), vii.

hundreds, of commercials with which the world bombards us. Each short-term thrill must lead to the next momentary payoff. Anything or anyone that gets in the way, be it my husband or wife, son or daughter, father or mother, the child in the womb, or God and the Church, must be moved along. The world tells us that all we need to feel worthwhile is one more luxury. Some people begin to believe that unless their lives have all the intensity of a music video they are somehow defective. And then they turn to drugs or other addictive behaviors to bring and sustain that intensity or to calm the hurt.

Society tells us if we could just do more things and do them all faster we would feel better. Several devices a day feed these messages to us, and we never once get insulted! Pope Benedict XVI has noted the irony that we seem to be afraid of disconnecting from the mass media even for a single moment.[27] These messages linger in our memory as we go to work, to school, and to practice. And what fills the thoughts sooner or later sinks into the heart. And the heart hardens. The advertisements and commercials become a series of commands by which we judge ourselves and measure others. And each advertisement leads us to spend more money, and more and more busyness to access its "promise" of happiness. Lastly, we begin to expect the same things from God. These worldly messages jam our radar for God and blind us to his movement of love.

The Ordinary Gift

As a result we often rush past the present moment. Our rushing makes a statement. We are saying that the present moment in each of our experiences is worthless, and even more, it is *in the way* and should be pushed aside. Of course, God has

---

27. See Pope Benedict XVI, *Verbum Domini*, 66.

other ideas about the present moment. After all, he created it. It is a gift. But happiness does not come through a television, computer, or cell phone. It comes only from God. He is the Creator of all matter and the hidden fullness of all motion. If we rush past the present moment, we rush past the sign of God's life and presence. In fact, in rushing past the present moment, we, in a sense, unwittingly "atheist-ize" the event and experience. We declare, indirectly, that God is *not* present to the ordinary and even tedious moments of life.

Within the ordinary, something always points to God, something that we can take to ourselves, or share with another in a legitimate and good way. It may take some docility to find it, but it is there. Saint Paul tells us, "Ever since the creation of the world his eternal power and divine nature, invisible though they are, have been understood and seen through the things he has made. So they are without excuse" (Rom 1:20). The great Cistercian Abbot and preacher Guerric of Igny tells us that the Holy Spirit makes a far deeper impression upon our hearts than material things can make on our senses.[28] Prayer transforms the interior noise into a conversation with God. In this endeavor, the inspired Word is the primary tool of the Holy Spirit. The first word of the entire Bible, the opening word of the Book of Genesis, is the word "When."[29] A theological assertion is at work here. God is eternal and thus wholly outside of, and free of, space and time, yet he creates both of them just as freely out of his generous love. Since God takes *time* to create, how can we rush past it? If we do, doesn't that

---

28. See Guerric of Igny, *Liturgical Sermons Book 2* (Kalamazoo, MI: Cistercian Publications, 1971), 83.

29. For an explanation of the Hebrew text, see Genesis: *The JPS Torah Commentary*, general editor and commentary by Nahum M. Sarna (Philadelphia: The Jewish Publication Society, 1989), 5.

rushing say something about our view of and reverence for God's creation? Space and time point beyond themselves to God. Every event and experience can draw us deeper into the love of God. If we expect perfection from ordinary events or experiences, we have in some measure declared them "not enough."

Space and time are meant to lead us to God. This does not mean we can skip Sunday Mass, or bypass the Sacrament of Penance or our own personal prayer. On the contrary, the ordinary events of life are meant to lead us to the sacraments, for a deeper and substantial sharing in God's life of grace. In ordinary events we are called to love of neighbor. These are not just polite manners. They can actually be *heroic* in some way. Often enough we tune out or rush past the ordinary delays and burdens of life to move rapidly on to what we feel is "really important" or what "really matters." We want to be with the "right crowd" and be at the center of the glitzy gathering, the fancier life, or the bigger payoff. Yet, when we do finally arrive at what we were speeding off to, we inevitably eventually discover disappointment and feel let down. This is often because we have hijacked the present moment of ordinary reality and exchanged it for a counterfeit and artificial venture that never arrives. We forfeit the original beauty of what *is*, for the counterfeit beauty of what *could be*. Why do we flee the ordinary? Could it be that the merely ordinary events and experiences of daily life remind us of how ordinary we are, and so we must speed past them all to keep up with our own ego and feel better inside?

Prayer with Sacred Scripture

Our heart is a very deep place. As we in docility accept the Holy Spirit's invitation, the light of Christ grows deeper within us.[30] As the prophet Isaiah tells us, "The LORD will be your everlasting light" (Is 60:20). The psalmist likewise says, "my God lights my darkness" (Ps 18:28), "You who are enthroned upon the cherubim, shine forth" (Ps 80:1), and God is "wrapped in light as with a garment" (Ps 104:2). The Gospels are the foundation of the dramatic "back and forth," the "to and fro" of concealment and revelation in which we see and grasp the God who, in his infinite freedom, makes himself *known* to us. In fact, it is *God* who grasps us. In the words of the sacred text God has spoken to us and continues to speak. He has disclosed something of his mystery to us and has done so definitively in the words and deeds of his Son Jesus Christ, especially in his saving passion, sacrificial death, and glorious resurrection. This is the definitive self-revelation of God to man. Our fear, once caught up in his sway, begins to waver and totter. Our sin is shown to be empty and futile. As we open the Scriptures we stumble upon the brink and threshold of love. His love *unravels* our fear, loosens and expands our heart, offers strength and forgiveness, and stirs us so that we become pliable, open to the innermost movements of his grace.

Throughout the Gospels Jesus leads us ever deeper. He is alluring. He appears preaching in the Temple area one day; the next he slips away in secret. One day he heals the sick or cures a leper, casts out a demon, and in the evening disputes with the Pharisees. The next day he astounds the crowd in response to a lawyer's quibble or a Pharisee's ongoing complaint. He turns water into wine, and he forgives sins.

Each time we read a passage of Scripture we find something new—a fresh, original, and deeper basis from which to

---

30. For a description of the Holy Spirit's work in our prayer see Hans Urs von Balthasar, *Christian Meditation* (San Francisco: Ignatius Press, 1989), 34. For the importance of docility, see Pope Benedict XVI, *Verbum Domini*, 6.

know and love God. What if we were to catch up with Jesus as he moves on from one town to the next? What if, as he strode along the road, we were to see our opportunity to catch up with him and look into his face? What if, at that moment, the pretense fell away? What if, for that moment, we interrupted him, took him by the elbow and gently directed him to the side of the road so we could talk? What would the curve of his cheek look like, or the color of his eyes? What would we think as the Maker of the universe, the God behind everything, looked back at us? What would we say? Would we tell him what we wanted, tell him our biggest problem? Would we want more? Whose name would we mention to him? Would we want him for what he could do for us, or would we in that moment perceive something more? What would he say in response? After our conversation, would we let him go on without us? Or would we follow? If so, where would he take us?

At times, we can meditate on messages *we want to hear*. But, as Pope Benedict XVI has pointed out, the word of God draws us into a *conversation* with Jesus.[31] Prayer gains access to the treasury of God's grace, which assists us to align our words of faith with moral action. We can build up expectations for highly personal, private feelings or sentiments that fill our prayer time. The pages that follow do not deny or even exclude this type of experience, but these meditations, rather than focusing on ourselves, center on Jesus and the message of the Gospel expressed in the authentic teaching of the Church. When we meet Jesus, his light illumines our darkness. The meditations that follow therefore also include a type of taking stock of the signs of the times, the trends and directions of the world that so often contradict God and his loving plan. As we approach the

---

31. See Pope Benedict XVI, *Verbum Domini*, 24.

word of God, the first movement is always one of humility of a simple faith. The *Catechism of the Catholic Church* emphasizes that humility is the very foundation of prayer.[32] Our meditation on the Gospel is never simply our private or prideful possession confined to our own internal experience; it leads us to plunge back into the darkness and bring the light of Christ to a world that is desperately searching for his love.

The Listener as a Hunter

When we pick up the Bible and begin to read it, or when we sit in the pew on Sunday listening to the readings, we are not simply passive. On the contrary, we are very active. In fact, we have to be like a *hunter*. The Dominican friar Humbert of Romans, as far back as the thirteenth century, compared the preacher to a hunter. Not only is the preacher a hunter, but so too is the person who listens to the Word proclaimed in church, or who reads the Scripture, as Saint Alphonsus Liguori emphasizes in his work *The Practice of the Love of Jesus*.[33] The Prophet Jeremiah said, "I will send for many hunters, and they shall hunt them from every mountain and every hill, and out of the clefts of the rocks" (Jer 16:16). When we listen to the words of Sacred Scripture, the Holy Spirit moves our hearts and inspires us to be patient and learn to listen. This is what a hunter does: The first skill of the hunter is patience. We may hear a phrase such as "The LORD is my shepherd, I shall not want" (Ps 23:1) or "Come to me, all you that are weary and are

---

32. *CCC*, no. 2559; See also Servais Pinckaers, OP, *The Sources of Christian Ethics* (Washington, DC: The Catholic University of America Press, 1995), 130, 228.

33. See Humbert of Romans, "Treatise on the Formation of Preachers" in *Early Dominicans: Selected Writings*. The Classics of Western Spirituality Series (Mahwah, NJ: Paulist Press, 1982), 191, and Saint Alphonsus de Liguori, "The Practice of the Love of Jesus" in *Alphonsus de Liguori Selected Writings*, 155.

carrying heavy burdens, and I will give you rest" (Mt 11:28). Phrases such as these open the trail to us. They linger in our heart. Just as the good hunter knows the path of his quarry, we know the paths where Jesus travels. And he is the One we are searching for.

These passages come back to our mind later during Mass, or later that day or during the week. That is not a mere coincidence but the Holy Spirit *reminding* us, helping us to turn the words over again and again to adapt them to our daily life. Some believers may feel that once they have left the church building on a Sunday, or finished saying a particular prayer, that the time of worship or prayer is done with and the obligation satisfied. But God wants and desires still more. The listener to the word of God is a hunter who must step out of predictable patterns, turn away from routine ideology, and escape from the obvious into recollection and meditation faithful to the genuine teaching of the Church.

The listener as a good hunter follows the subtle signs of the trail of truth. Instead of hoping that the readings at Mass won't be too long, we should find a way to disappear into the Scripture passage, camouflaged and still, careful and absorbed. Like the hunter, we *wait*. We disappear *into the passage* so as to *wait for God*. We know he is near as we listen with an open heart, waiting for that word or phrase that really captures our hearing or echoes back for us. We have to be heedful of signs, tracks, predictable patterns; we evaporate into the shadows of the passage and track down traces of the Spirit that others easily pass over. Think of the hunter: He gets dirty and wet, and he hides not out of fear but out of expectancy. So too must we as we listen to the Word proclaimed or read Scripture. We read not for information but for the gentle, and sometimes not so gentle, nudge of God's forming hand. We must develop an instinct for the Word we hear. We pass over the same passages time and again until they become familiar terrain and well-trodden paths.

Likewise, we sense our own fears and burdens. We know our pain and bewilderment, which can easily hide behind the pleasantries we exchange with others. Over time our memory lends us agility so we follow the trail of a Scripture passage and are also aware of the daily traps we face. Each word we hear has a particular weight. Each word can open a door into meditation because these are the words of the Holy Spirit. As the *Catechism of the Catholic Church* teaches, "The Holy Spirit gives a spiritual understanding of the word of God to those who read or hear it, according to the dispositions of their hearts."[34]

The Holy Spirit longs to guide us into the ultimate ground of the mysteries of Jesus, those of his public ministry, and most centrally his Paschal Mystery, his passion, death, and resurrection. As with hearing the word proclaimed during Mass, the pages that follow are meant to lead us somewhere: to the encounter with Christ in the sacraments. And that encounter then leads us deeper into his word, Sacred Scripture, so that we meet Christ all the more deeply and are led to serve our neighbor in love.

So, as we enter the passage of Sacred Scripture, we want to find a place that will be quiet for even a few short moments: perhaps the final ten minutes of a lunch hour, or while the baby naps, or while waiting in the doctor's office. It might even be at the end of the day, just before bed. Steal a few moments and give them to God who is sure to be present. We are not very used to stillness, especially inner stillness.[35] As we turn to the practice of prayer, we can be sure that it will involve self-denial

---

34. *CCC*, no. 1101.

35. See Hans Urs von Balthasar, *Christian Meditation*, 18.

and openness to the movement of the Holy Spirit. As we make this turn, we draw upon and renew the act of faith made in our baptism. Through the pages that follow may we allow the Holy Spirit to make room in our heart, so that his grace can form and sharpen us, and transform us through and through in the sacraments so that the unmistakable and indescribable beauty of Christ may radiate light to the world.

CHAPTER ONE

The Annunciation

In the sixth month the angel Gabriel was sent by God to a town in Galilee called Nazareth, to a virgin engaged to a man whose name was Joseph, of the house of David. The virgin's name was Mary. (Lk 1:26–27)

The movement itself is almost imperceptible.[1] Not quite invisible, it is remarkably real. It resembles the petals of a new spring bud that depart one another's embrace in open flower. It has all the fanfare of a distant ripple in a small corner of a large lake. Like the opening note of a symphony, something new is in motion. The large stretch of eternity firmly

---

1. Hans Urs von Balthasar notes that Our Lady's experience is at once so deeply secret and so profoundly rich that it virtually defies description (See Hans Urs von Balthasar, *The Glory of the Lord: A Theological Aesthetics I: Seeing the Form* [San Francisco: Ignatius Press, 1989], 338).

reaches into "the sixth month." The vast span of eternity intersects with time in the smallest of moments. Time blushes at eternity. Each respects the other, neither overtakes the other, yet both surrender. Time has found all it ever wanted in eternity, and eternity in time. At this fruitful juncture, an angel's voice is heard. And this almost imperceptible movement that exceeds all meaning takes place "in the sixth month."

It seems impossible, doesn't it? That something moves in heaven, and we know about it on earth. It seems fine as long as we keep it wrapped up in church. But, once we take it outside the church building, or so we think, it should separate and evaporate. What does all of this have to do with our daily lives? Science should be among the first, not the last, to see. After all, science explores space, time, matter, motion—and light. Light is one of the names for God (see Jn 1:4–9; 8:12; 1 Jn 1:5; Jas 1:17).

Heaven is when light
gets its voice and its say
And, poised, this galaxy of bright sound
Tells the detailed reason of the meadows it has inched across,
       alone;
And kept its data to ferment

And tells the full affair of
One-hundred ocean waves it briefly kissed,
and ridden wait-less, hitching one to another
to some shore obscure
in the height of a momentary lapped existence, it reveals
the seeing of a different sort.

Its faithful sport, light
Never gives up
Making things
Known.

Even dark. Even here.

Gathered in from the ocean,
And deserting the meadows it stands
With all the speed of obedience ready
For night's harshest wait-less demands:

Even now foreshadows cast, its tongue speaks smarts
To bring a child's stamps to whimper
Like some intelligent spell
Comprehended at its casting having mercy on the crib, beneath.

Where does light learn its lesson?

In a moment for all time . . . What hides behind the light
  is brighter still.

The witnesses knew:
You saw an angel the last time you saw light
Did you listen?

Something moved in heaven: "the angel Gabriel was sent *from God. . . .*" The words may seem incidental, but they are anything but incidental: Heaven moved. And God, the almighty, eternal, invisible God, *sent* an angel.

We are not comfortable with angels. We put them through an obstacle course to make them conform to our expectations. True witnesses, they flunk our course. If we cannot see something under a microscope or through a telescope, we arbitrarily declare that it does not exist. We do not detect the angel through the lens of a microscope or telescope. Rather we catch a passing hint and vanishing clue of the angel's work in the light of truth by which we make the telescope and microscope. Saint Augustine of Hippo explains that when God said, "Let there be light" (Gn 1:3), this refers to the very creation of the angels.[2] Unlike God, our world has largely given up on angels.

Fortunately the angels have not given up on us. It is rather ironic for the contemporary world to say that because God and angels are not visible, they do not exist, when that same contemporary world invests billions of dollars and countless hours in video games, reality television, and advertising which, while visible, are meaningless and fleeting. Visibility, it seems, cannot be the criterion for meaning and existence. On occasion those who declare themselves to be people of science turn aside from religion and cite those times in history when people have done terrible things in the name of religion or the Church. Based on these events, the world seems to find it easy to stop listening to the Church. The tragic actions that some religious people have done purportedly in the name of the Church are not actions of the Church, but of sinful individuals. That some erroneous people do horrendous things in the name of the Church does not in any way disprove the Church's divine mission. If anything, it reveals how much we need the Church in all of her authentic and lasting beauty.

The same is true of science. People of faith do not stop believing in the authentic importance of science because some scientists found a way to build a nuclear bomb, abort the child in the womb, create chemical weapons, euthanize human beings, or assist with suicide. Such acts do not tell us to abandon or reject science, but reveal how much we actually need ethical and sound science in the first place. There is a considerable difference between science itself and what some people do in its name. So too with the Church.

Something moves in heaven and a region of light opens up on earth. "This is the message we have heard from him and

---

2. Saint Augustine, *City of God*, book XI, chapter IX.

proclaim to you, that God is light and in him there is no darkness at all" (1 Jn 1:5). He is "the Father of lights, with whom there is no variation or shadow due to change" (Jas 1:17). The psalmist proclaimed: "In your light we see light" (Ps 36:9). The prophet Baruch proclaims, "[He] sends forth the light, and it goes; he called it, and it obeyed him, trembling" (Bar 3:33).

Saint John tells us, "[I]n him was life, and the life was the light of all people. The light shines in the darkness, and the darkness did not overcome it" (Jn 1:4–5). When God communicates his light, the expanse of light is compact, deep, and dense. Saint Gregory the Great tells us that the angels, essentially invisible beings, become visible through their *beauty*, names, and ministries.[3] The region of light, as it enters space, takes place as an event that takes form in time itself. Prepared from the first moment of her existence, Mary's deepest intuition stirs. She has no resistance to this visit of light. The light has been freely drawn to her mystery, as if the prophet Isaiah were speaking of this very moment: "the LORD will arise upon you, and his glory will appear over you" (Is 60:2).

The dawning movement disturbs nothing. The doorway to the Blessed Virgin Mary's home in Nazareth is the threshold between eternity and time: An angel on one side, the Blessed Virgin "betrothed to a man named Joseph" (see Lk 1:27 NAB) on the other. The angel crosses. The silence only deepens as the light heightens and crests at Mary's reception. The expansive moment opens wide without ever losing its quality of near and almost practical imperceptibility. This event is at once so honestly luminous, radiant, and real that it has a name: Gabriel.

And God, from the heart of his eternity, has sent this angel Gabriel as a messenger, a courier, "to a town in Galilee called Nazareth" (Lk 1:26). When we are speaking of God and angels

---

3. Saint Gregory the Great, *Homily* 34, Sections 7 and 9.

and eternity, why do we need to speak of a region and town by name? True brilliance is attracted to the humble, and the humble are nearly imperceptible. The smaller things are on earth, the larger they are in God. As the prophet Isaiah said, "The least of them shall become a clan, and the smallest one a mighty nation; I am the LORD; in its time I will accomplish it quickly" (Is 60:22). Gabriel announced the birth of Saint John the Baptist to his father Zachariah in the sanctuary of the temple (see Lk 1:13). Gabriel announces the birth of the Savior in the sanctuary of the home—the home of the Virgin Mary. The grace of God is not confined to the temple, but reaches, and in a sense, establishes its profound center in the home. Already the words of the psalmist are being fulfilled, "All the ends of the earth have seen the victory of our God" (Ps 98:3). We go as well in the one small movement from the immensity of eternity to the specific local address of "a virgin betrothed." Like it has with angels, our world has also largely given up on virginity. Like the angels, fortunately, virginity has not given up on us.

"The virgin's name was Mary" (Lk 1:27). What was almost imperceptible a moment before is now very specific. Something moved in heaven: a shift, an opening, whose only source can be love. The Big Bang pays attention and bows at this magnificence. Such is the humility of God and the elaborate silence of love. From eternity, God sent the angel Gabriel into time to a region and town of this world, to the Virgin Mary who was betrothed to a man named Joseph. God acted. When God acts, his greatest acts are almost imperceptible. They are barely a ripple. The more invisible the action of God seems, the more real it is. The more distant the action of God seems, the closer it is. Isaiah the prophet summed it up: "For my thoughts are not your thoughts, nor are your ways my ways, says the LORD" (Is 55:8), and again, "[T]he LORD does not see as mortals see; they look on the outward appearance, but the

LORD looks on the heart" (1 Sam 16:7). God, who is love, always sees and abides in authentic truth. This is why love suffers. Love alone spans eternal truth into time. And so, love suffers.[4]

> And he came to her and said, "Greetings, favored one! The Lord is with you." (Lk 1:28)

Light becomes sound. Brilliance ignites into words, which portend a heavenly avalanche. The perfect angelic knowledge of Gabriel meets the perfect humility of Mary. Angels speak all the time. Whereas only true charity can hear the voice of the angel, only humility can understand the angelic words. Pride is therefore the leading cause of spiritual deafness. Untreated, pride hardens the heart and crushes the spirit. The sin of pride cannot be tamed. It must be killed off in us, extinguished. Only the rare vintage of grace called humility can overtake the venom of vanity and pride. Heaven's first movement is always "humility."

The angel's words bring heavenly news. We know all too well what it's like to receive bad news. We hear of house fires, cancer, and drive-by shootings. Bad news travels quickly, usually by the express route of gossip. Gossip even converts good news for someone else into bad news with the phrase: "Well, you know why *that* happened. . . ." The psalmist alerts us to the wickedness that can flow from the tongue: "[T]he scheming of evildoers, who whet their tongues like swords, who aim bitter words like arrows, shooting from ambush at the blameless . . ." (Ps 64:2–4). The great saints warn us about the evil of gossip. Saint Paul exhorts us, "Let no one deceive you with empty words" (Eph 5:6). Saint Anthony of the Desert meditates on the words of the Book

---

4. On this, see Pope Benedict XVI, *Dogma and Preaching: Applying Christian Doctrine to Daily Life*, first unabridged edition (San Francisco: Ignatius Press, 2011), 95–96.

of Proverbs: "The mouths of fools are their ruin" (Prov 18:7). Saint Anthony warns us that evil speech is the worst of poisons. He further notes that those who gossip often whisper, and that if we allow the whisperer to even approach us he will take every merit away from us.[5] Recall the parable Jesus told about the rich man. Tormented in flames, he asked Abraham to send Lazarus to dip his finger in water and cool the rich man's tongue (see Lk 16:24). Saint Gregory the Great explains that besides his neglect of the poor, this man's sin was talkativeness.[6] Spiritual writers also warn us about the danger of gossip's first cousin: idle conversation. Several of the late medieval mystics tell us that when we refrain from idle speech the Lord desires to give us greater rewards than if we were to fast for seven years on bread and water without giving up idle conversation.[7] Such talk is empty conversation, which brings a void into the space where only a blessing should be.[8] Turning away from this fault is even more difficult today, since our endless 24/7 news drones on and on.

Angels have spoken to human beings before, but what follows next is unlike any conversation in history: "Greetings, favored one! The Lord is with you." The theological writer Origen declares that he could not find such a greeting anywhere else in all of Sacred Scripture.[9] Gabriel's words, along with Saint Elizabeth's (see Lk 1:42), form the words of the

---

5. Saint Anthony, *Watchfulness of the Tongue*, PG 40, col. 965.

6. See Saint Gregory the Great, *Moralia in Job*, vol. 1, book 1, chapter 11.

7. See Nicolas of Strasbourg, *The Sermon on the Golden Mountain* in *Late Medieval Mysticis of the Low Countries*. The Classics of Western Spirituality Series (Mahwah, NJ: Paulist Press, 2008), 57.

8. See Adrienne von Speyr, *The Letter to the Ephesians* (San Francisco: Ignatius Press, 1996), 197, 208.

9. Origen, "Homily on the Gospel of Luke, 6.7," in *Homilies on Luke, Fathers of the Church: A New Translation*, vol. 94 (Washington, DC: The Catholic University of America Press, 2009).

"Hail Mary"—the most quoted and repeated greeting in history. Every recitation of the Rosary repeats this greeting over fifty times. In prayer we take the words of the angel as our own.[10] The words of the Hail Mary, which proclaim the plan of God and the birth of his Son, in a sense introduce the Our Father, which the Son himself gives to us. The Hail Mary and the Our Father are intimately connected.

The magnitude of Gabriel's greeting speaks volumes. The Greek word used in the Scripture passage for "full of grace" is *kecharitōmenē*. This word speaks of Mary as the recipient of God's action: Our Lady has already been blessed or graced in a permanent and complete manner by the action of God. Mary is to be the Mother of God. In the plan of God, it is most appropriate and fitting that Mary is therefore free from Original Sin and that her most sublime holiness is resplendent in the plan of God. Mary is immaculate, the spotless pure Virgin undefiled by sin. The Church teaches that Our Lady is the Immaculate Conception. Mary is preserved from all stain of sin by a singular grace from God, from the first moment of her conception in the womb of her mother, Saint Anne. God accomplishes this in Mary by applying to her the merits of the cross of Jesus. Love creates time; therefore love can apply the highest gift of love, the sacrifice of Jesus on the cross, to any moment in history, before, during, or since the sacrifice of the cross. Mary is free from sin due to the action of Jesus.

> But She was much perplexed (*dietarachthē*) by his words and pondered (*dielogizeto*) what sort of greeting this might be. (Lk 1:29)

The original Greek further opens the passage to our understanding: "And when she saw (*idousa*) him she was troubled

---

10. See *CCC*, no. 2676.

(*dietarachthē*) at his saying."[11] Notice that Luke emphasizes that Mary *sees* (*idousa*) the angel. On one level she sees the angel through her visual perception; on a deeper level she sees by faith. Mary's experience with the angel is not simply the imparting of information. In the mystery of the annunciation, Mary encounters the angel and *sees* the plan of God in the angel's message. She *sees* and beholds the divine illumination of the mission of salvation, and this brilliance gives shape, as it has from the first moment of her conception, to her very being.

In the tradition, *seeing* is a kind of knowing and believing.[12] The message of the angel is not simply a clarification or explanation of what is about to take place. It is an all-encompassing act, the final unveiling of congruence between the message of the angel and the person of the Blessed Mother. Like meets like. God bestows and Mary receives, *takes in to herself* all that is true about her very existence and mission. This reception is Mary's humble response of faith that immediately trusts and grasps the mysterious depths of the divine illumination. Because of her immaculate heart, Mary always senses immediately the unsurpassable truth.[13] Yet notice her overriding humility. Saint Bernard of Clairvaux tells us that the Blessed Virgin Mary is so noble that she is greeted by an angel and yet so humble as to be the fiancée of a workman.[14]

The Gospel passage emphasizes that in the moment she sees the angel, Our Lady is troubled at his words. Her Son too will be troubled. The word used to describe Mary in this verse

---

11. Because of some slight variations in the Greek wording of this text, not all manuscripts have the word *idousa*. The verse with *idousa* is from a Byzantine text of the Gospel of Saint Luke.

12. See Hans Urs von Balthasar, *The Glory of the Lord I*, 141.

13. Ibid., 362.

14. See Saint Bernard of Clairvaux, *Homilies in Praise of the Virgin Mother* (Kalamazoo, MI: Cistercian Publications, 1993), 9.

as troubled (*dietarachthē*) is also used to describe the emotion of Jesus as troubled in spirit when he approaches the tomb of his friend Lazarus (see Jn 11:33). The same word is also used when Jesus faces his hour of the cross (see Jn 12:27) and when Jesus tells his apostles that one of them would betray him (see Jn 13:21).[15] Our Lady is already sharing in the mission of her Son. At the same time, the inward commotion or distress (*dietarachthē*) that Mary experiences differs somewhat from the agony that her Son will experience later in the Gospel of Luke. In the Garden of Olives Jesus will suffer agony (*agōnia*), which comes from the word for a struggle for victory in a contest or trial, as in an arena. In the agony in the garden, Jesus experiences severe mental anguish. In that moment an angel from heaven appears and strengthens the Lord (see Lk 22:43).

Mary's response to the trouble is to ponder. Already she is showing us, her children, how to respond in moments of trouble and distress. The word for ponder, *dielogizeto*, means to turn something over in the mind. Mary looks for connections in what she has seen and heard, in order to reason, consider, and muse within her heart.

Yet, as is always the case with the Blessed Mother, more is taking place.

A greeting is the first word of another by which we are *drawn to* that other. Mary hears the first word of the angel, and in a sense she *sees* the first word of the angel in the light of the angel's very presence. Mary's calmness of mind is stirred up or disturbed (*dietarachthē*). The rousing spoken of here does not seem to be a negative upsetting or agitation but rather a positive stirring forth and an enthusing. Indeed the root word here is

---

15. See Pope Benedict XVI, *Jesus of Nazareth Part Two, Holy Week: From the Entrance into Jerusalem to the Resurrection* (San Francisco: Ignatius Press, 2011), Kindle Edition, chapter 6.2, loc. 2059 of 4202.

the same one found in the passage in Saint John's Gospel in which the angel troubles (*tarachthē*) the waters at the pool of Bethesda (see Jn 5:4, 7), and the waters, once troubled, heal.

The early Fathers of the Church saw the baptismal font as the womb of the Church. Just as the Holy Spirit overshadowed the womb of Mary, so too, the baptismal font is a womb for members of the Church. Saint Leo the Great says, "the water of baptism is like the Virgin's womb, for the same Holy Spirit fills the font, who filled the Virgin."[16] In this sense, in the present passage the angel may be said to be troubling or stirring the waters of Mary's spirit as God's final preparation for the over-shadowing of the Holy Spirit (see Lk 1:35), so that lasting healing may come forth in the Incarnation of the Word made flesh (see Jn 1:14). And Mary meditates, contemplating what she has seen and heard. She immediately turns in humility and seeks to discover the hidden meaning even in what seems per-plexing and confounding. *This is humility in motion*: Mary does not refer the mystery of what she has heard to *herself* but to *God*. In the brilliance of the angel's light Our Lady searches for even more light. Balthasar reminds us that the first gift of light is humility.[17] Humility is the sense organ of the human heart. Nothing can enter our heart except through the light of humil-ity. If we do not have humility, our heart is hardened.

The greatest "proofs" for the existence of God do not come from arguments or explanations, but from humility. Atheists commonly refer to the Christian's concept of belief in God as a convoluted coping mechanism built on the denial of death. Yet, the atheists' mistake is failing to see that their own denial

---

16. Saint Leo the Great, Sermon 24.3, P. Schaff et al., eds. *A Select Library of the Nicene and Post-Nicene Fathers of the Christian Church* (Grand Rapids, MI: Wm. B. Eerdmans Publishing Company, 1969), II, 12:135.

17. See Hans Urs von Balthasar, *The Glory of the Lord I*, 163.

of God is a belief *in* death. Humility always believes in *life*. Humility transforms all that we encounter so that the heart can receive it. In the words of the angel, light became sound only to again become light in the heart of the humble Virgin. We think of the words of the psalmist: "Deep calls to deep" (Ps 42:7). Humility invites. Usually the greeting of the "greeter" draws in the one greeted. Here it is reversed: the angel greets, but it is Our Lady who draws in the angel. Angels rush to humility's side.

> Then the angel said to her, "Do not be afraid, Mary, for you have found favor with God." (Lk 1:30)

The angel responds: "Do not be afraid (*mē phobou*) . . . for you have found (*heures*) favor with God." While the word fear (*phobou*) certainly can mean "to be terrified or alarmed," it seems likely that its other meaning as "reverence" or "awe" is highlighted in this context. In a sense, the angel is reflecting that Mary is not to be in awe of him; instead, the angel is in awe of Mary.

We have many ways of approaching God. We call out to him. We petition him. We plead with him and praise him, which is all very fitting and essential to our life of prayer. But we have it on the authority of an angel that humility, above all else, *finds* God. Mary, the lowly Virgin of Nazareth, has not only found favor with God; she has *found* God. In the very moment that the mystery is announced and begins to unfold, Our Lady entrusts herself to it with immediate freedom and completeness, that is to say, with full humility and total obedience.

Unlike the angel at the empty tomb who tells the women not to be afraid (see Mt 28:5, Mk 16:6), Gabriel's words "Do not be afraid" are not an instance of the angel giving advice to Mary. Rather, Gabriel *describes what he sees in Mary*: "Fear not!" He uses the imperative or command form of speech, which shows that

Our Lady's humility is strong and immediate, not vague or hesitant. True humility, contrary to the world's poor caricature of it, is not fearful or tentative, because humility frees us from trouble. In fact, true humility does not fear: it is steadfast and strong, but it need not show off its strength because its strength comes from its silence, grows in its stillness, and blossoms in its calm.

> "Behold you will conceive in your womb and bear a son, and you shall name him Jesus. He will be great and will be called Son of the Most High, and the Lord God will give him the throne of David his father, and he will rule over the house of Jacob forever, and of his kingdom there will be no end." (Lk 1:31–33, NAB)

And the strength comes forth: "Behold." The words of the angel are words of praise, rather than simply words of explanation. Angels unceasingly praise and worship God. Gabriel speaks clearly every syllable of heaven's highest secret, the great mystery over which the angelic world marvels: "Behold you will conceive in your womb and bear a son, and you shall name Him Jesus. He will be great and will be called Son of the Most High, and the Lord God will give him the throne of David his father, and he will rule over the house of Jacob forever, and of his kingdom there will be no end" (Lk 1:31–33 NAB).

Balthasar says that this verse is the first formal and explicit biblical revelation of the Trinity.[18] He notes that the dialogue with the angel has three successive stages. First, Gabriel announces: "The Lord is with you" second, "you shall bear a *Son* who shall be called the Son of the Most High"; and third, "the *Holy Spirit* will overshadow you" (see Lk 1:28–35). This leads to "the mystery hidden for ages in God who created all things"

---

18. Hans Urs von Balthasar, *Explorations in Theology I: The Word Made Flesh* (San Francisco: Ignatius Press, 1989), 197.

(Eph 3:9; see Col 1:26). The Second Person of the Most Blessed Trinity, the eternal Son of God, will take to himself a true human nature, without ceasing to be God. He will do so through being conceived in the womb of the Blessed Virgin Mary and so he will be the Author of our salvation. His name, "Jesus," means "one who saves." Jesus is not just a good man. He is not just a teacher of a way of life like other teachers in history. Jesus is the only Son of God and Savior of the world. He does not simply give advice; he saves the world from sin and death, and in doing so he reveals the Father in the Holy Spirit. The child conceived and born of Mary is truly the eternal God: without ceasing to be God, he became true man in the womb of the Virgin Mary.

On the Feast of the Annunciation, March 25, the Church celebrates the wonder of the unsearchable depths of the Incarnation. Venerable Bede emphasizes that through the action of the Holy Spirit, "Jesus, that is, our Savior, was both the true Son of God the Father and the true Son of a mother who was a human being."[19] As Saint Augustine said, he who in his divine nature is the equal of the Father assumed the condition of a slave and became like us, and so restored to us our likeness to God. The only Son of God became a son of man to make many men sons of God.[20] The Doctor of Grace further notes, "the blessed and beatific God, having become a participant in our humanity, has offered a shorter route to participation in his divinity."[21]

The mystery that Jesus was truly conceived of the Virgin Mary without the introduction of the male seed does not

---

19. Venerable Bede, *Homilies on the Gospels* (Kalamazoo, MI: Cistercian Studies, 1973), Cistercian Studies 110, 22.

20. Saint Augustine, *Sermon* 194, 3–4: PL 38, 1016–1017.

21. Saint Augustine, *City of God*, book IX, chapter XV.

denigrate human sexuality. Rather, it demonstrates to us the mystery that Jesus is truly God and truly man. If Jesus had been born of Saint Joseph, then Jesus would only be man. If Jesus had not been truly born of Mary, then Jesus would only be God. He took his humanity from the Virgin Mary: the blood that the Son shed on Calvary has its ultimate human source from Mary. The Son of God, a divine Person, has taken to himself a real humanity in the Incarnation.

Because human nature and divine nature are united in the Person of the Word in the womb of the Virgin Mary, the saints have referred to her womb as a nuptial chamber. There, the marriage of human and divine nature in the Son of God took place.[22] This miraculous union came about when Mary was betrothed to Saint Joseph, the foster father of Jesus. Marriage is thus also greatly exalted by the coming of the Savior to the world. Saint Joseph, too, learned of the incarnation through the word of an angel:

> Now the birth of Jesus the Messiah took place in this way. When his mother Mary had been engaged to Joseph, but before they lived together, she was found to be with child from the Holy Spirit. Her husband Joseph, being a righteous (*dikaios*) and unwilling to expose her to public disgrace, planned to dismiss (*apolysai*) her quietly (*lathra*).
>
> But just when he had resolved to do this, an angel of the Lord appeared to him in a dream and said, 'Joseph, son of David, do not be afraid to take Mary as your wife, for the child conceived in her is from the Holy Spirit. She will bear a son, and you are to name him Jesus, for he will save his people from their sins.' All this took place to fulfill what had been spoken by the Lord through the prophet: "Look, the

---

22. See Saint Augustine, *On the Psalms*, Philip Schaff, ed. *Nicene and Post Nicene Fathers* vol. 8 (Peabody, MA: Hendrickson Publishers, 2004), Ps XLV. 3; 146. For marriage as a symbol of the redemption, see Hans Urs von Balthasar, *Explorations in Theology II: Spouse of the Word* (San Francisco: Ignatius Press, 1991), 188.

virgin shall conceive and bear a son, and they shall name him Emmanuel," which means, "God is with us." (Mt 1:18–25)

Notice the difference in the way the angel appears to Our Lady and the way that he appears to Saint Joseph. The angel comes to Mary during the day, "in the sixth month." The angel comes to Joseph in a dream, presumably at night. The difference in timing reflects a deeper difference. Our Lady, without sin, sees directly, in the light of day. Joseph, not free from sin, experiences the word of God through sleep, a type of visionary contemplation.

We tend to interpret the angel's words to Joseph as meaning that he was confused at Mary's pregnancy, since she was found with child after they were betrothed but before they came together. We also tend to think that the angel had to convince Joseph not to divorce Mary, and to explain to him the plan of God that Joseph had unwittingly ventured upon.

However, another interpretation is possible.[23] Matthew describes Joseph as a righteous man (*dikaios*). A righteous man is blameless (see Gn 6:9), hates falsehood (see Prv 13:5), and walks in integrity (see Prv 20:7). But he also "falls seven times a day and rises again" (Prv 24:16 NAB). The prayer of the righteous man accomplishes much (see Jas 5:16). The righteous man is learned (see Prv 9:9): he knows the Scriptures. He knows the prophecy that the messiah will be born of a virgin who will conceive and bear a son (see Is 7:14). Joseph also knows the blessedness of Mary, his betrothed. Far from suspecting

---

23. See Saint Thomas Aquinas, *STh* Supplement, IIIa, q 62, 3 ad 2, and Saint Bernard, *In Praise of the Virgin* Mary, Sermon 2, 14. See also René Laurentin, *The Truth of Christmas: Beyond the Myths* (Still River, MA: Saint Bede Publications), 265 ff; John Saward, *Redeemer in the Womb* (San Francisco: Ignatius Press, 1993), 38–42; and Jean Daniélou, *The Infancy Narratives* (New York: Herder and Herder, 1968), 40. See also Ignance de la Potterie, SJ, *Mary in the Mystery of the Covenant* (New York: Alba House, 1992), 37ff.

anything untoward about her, he does suspect that God is at work in Mary. The angel is sent to confirm this. The phrase "expose her to shame" (*deigmatisai*) comes from the root word "to show forth" (*deigma*) (to display openly or to expose to the eyes). Saint Joseph was unwilling to expose, display, or show forth the mystery of Mary to the eyes of others. Humility was the basis of his fear. He knew God was acting in Mary, and the Gospel tells us that he wanted to "withdraw" (*apolysai*) from her "quietly" (*lathra*) (see Mt 1:19).

Although the word *apolysai* can at times mean divorce, it has a deeper meaning more true to the present context: to set free and to hold back no longer. In this passage, divorce does not seem to be its meaning because at that time one could not divorce quietly. Once had to give a public writ of divorce (see Mt 19:7; Dt 24:1–4). If he expected something untoward, a righteous man such as Saint Joseph would *have had to* follow the law, which did not allow a quiet divorce in the civil sense. From the text and the context, rather, it seems very likely that Joseph in his humility was secretly trying to escape notice, to release Mary, to free her from himself,[24] and so be hidden from her great and overwhelming mystery. This same root word for "quietly" (*lathra*) is used to describe what Jesus did when, in the midst of his public ministry, he "went away to the region of Tyre. He entered a house and did not want anyone to know he was there. Yet he could not escape notice" (Mk 7:24).

Saint Luke also uses this word to describe the action of the woman with the hemorrhage whom Jesus heals: "When the woman saw that she could not remain hidden, she came trembling; and falling down before him, she declared in the presence of all the people why she had touched him, and how she had been immediately healed" (Lk 8:47).

---

24. See *STh* Supplement, IIIa, q62, 3 ad 2.

Saint John uses this same word to describe the intention of Pilate during Our Lord's trial: As he hears those who have handed over refer to the Lord as the "Son of God" and as he himself questions Jesus, Pilate is increasingly troubled and begins to sense the great mystery of Jesus Christ. And so, Pilate seeks to *apolysō* or "release" Jesus, to send him away and so gain distance from the mystery before him. So too, the angel does not come to talk Saint Joseph out of divorce, but to strengthen him and confirm his humility before the mystery of God, which is taking place in his midst.

A nightly mission, the operative at last dispatched
    from the
real to unreal world.
The angel enters the corridors of sleep where the troubled
    Joseph rests;
Interrupting one wonder with Another
whispering the long-treasured saving Plan,
prophecy becomes reality as
A seer's vision brims.

Joseph's sleep continues in the wake of the Almighty
At the noiseless morning breaking (or is that sin's back?)
the angel close to now returned to his haven, glances round
And sees as Joseph stands and stretches
the preview of Another Rising much more final and profound.

Mary said to the angel, "How can this be, since I am a virgin?" The angel said to her, "The Holy Spirit will come upon you, and the power of the Most High will overshadow you; therefore the child to be born will be holy; he will be called Son of God. And now, your relative Elizabeth in her old age has also conceived a son; and this is the sixth month for her who was said to be barren. For nothing will be impossible with God." (Lk 1:34–37)

Mary's first words to the angel are, in one sense, not for her own benefit, but for ours:[25] "How can this be, since I have no relations with a man?" Mary allows us to learn the mystery of her divine motherhood and of her perpetual virginity from the angel. The angel moves to the heart of the mystery: "The Holy Spirit will come upon you, and the power of the Most High will overshadow you." The Old Testament describes a variety of holy realities, such as the Sabbath (see Ex 16:23), the holy place (see Ex 26:33; 28:29), and holy things (see Ex 28:38, 31:10, 35:21; Lv 5:15). The Holy Spirit is the Third Person of the Most Blessed Trinity, coequal and coeternal with the Father and the Son. The second verse of the book of Genesis tells us that in God's original creative act, "the earth was a formless void and darkness covered the face of the deep, while a wind from God swept over the face of the waters." (Gn 1:2). The Hebrew word for "wind" is *ruach*. In Greek, this word is translated as *pneuma;* in Latin, *spiritus;* and in English, *spirit*, for Holy Spirit. Just as a wind is an invisible power, so too, the Holy Spirit manifests the invisible power of God.[26]

In creating man, God *breathes* the breath of life into him (see Gn 2:7). God is present to the prophet Elijah in the whispering sound (see 1 Kgs 19:12), and later takes Elijah to heaven in a whirlwind (see 2 Kgs 2:1, 11). The psalmist says of God, "You make the clouds your chariot, you ride on the wings of the wind" (Ps 104:3). The Lord Jesus proclaims to Nicodemus, "The wind blows where it chooses, and you hear the sound of it, but you do not know where it comes from or where it goes. So it is with everyone who is born of the Spirit" (Jn 3:8).

---

25. See John Saward, *Cradle of Redeeming Love: The Theology of the Christmas Mystery* (San Francisco: Ignatius Press, 2002), 218.

26. See Pope John Paul II, *God: Father and Creator: A Catechesis on the Creed* (Boston: Pauline Books & Media, 1996), 173; see also Prosper Grech, *An Outline of New Testament Spirituality,* 92.

The angel declares that the power of the Most High will overshadow (*episkiasei*) Mary. The word "overshadow" likewise conveys a particular form of the presence and action of the otherwise invisible power of God, manifested through the presence and action of the Holy Spirit. Unlike an ordinary shadow that blocks light, the overshadowing action of God concentrates the light. The prophet proclaims, "His glory covered the heavens, and the earth was full of his praise. The brightness was like the sun" (Hab 3:3–4).

As a shadow of light, not darkness, the divine shadow illuminates. When God overshadows, the divine shadow covers an area that belongs especially to God, the place where God has chosen to dwell. In the Book of Exodus, the glory of the LORD appeared in the cloud (see Ex 16:10). Likewise, the cloud that overshadowed the temple was the sign of the presence of the Lord: "Then the cloud covered the tent of meeting, and the glory of the LORD filled the tabernacle" (Ex 40:34).[27] The angel proclaims that the presence of God, as it once overshadowed the tent of meeting, will overshadow Mary. The glory of the Lord will now dwell in Mary in an unprecedented way, for Our Lady is to be the Mother of God's only begotten Son. The presence of God in the womb of Mary points immediately to the doctrine of Mary's perpetual virginity. Our Lady is ever-virgin. She is a virgin before (*ante partum*), during (*in partu*), and ever-after (*et post partum*) the birth of Jesus. Saint Leo the Great emphasizes that the birth of Jesus goes beyond human understanding and surpasses all precedent.[28] This is

---

27. For the significance of the image of the cloud as an element of theophanies, see Xavier Léon-Dufour, *Resurrection and the Message of Easter* (New York: Holt, Rinehart, and Winston, 1975), 34.

28. See Pope Leo I, *Sermons, Fathers of the Church: A New Translation* (Washington, DC: The Catholic University of America Press, 1996), vol. 93, 128–129.

because she is the Ark of the New Covenant, the place where only God may dwell.

The same word "overshadow" is used to describe what happens to Jesus when Saint John the Baptist baptizes him in the Jordan River (see Mk 9:7). It is also used in relation to the bright cloud that covers the apostles at the transfiguration (see Mt 17:5; Lk 9:34), and to Peter's shadow that falls on the sick in the streets, that they may be healed (see Acts 5:15).

> *Humanity in such a tangled snare*
> *. . . where did this all come from?*
> *A warning rises*
> *A prophet's voice*
> *"WATCH" into the darkness*
> *A people called again to turn an eager, weary head*
> *In a resistant time*
> *To look through the darkness of a Judean night and*
> *Trust that in the darkness of a Virgin's womb*
> *The Creator of Light begins to form.*
>
> *As Advent begins, watch now and trust that*
> *In your own unfamiliar darkness—*
> *Inadequacy, job loss, depression, or distance*
> *There is a taste of the Bethlehem darkness,*
> *Containing a flavor of the Promise*
> *A Savior already forming from the Overshadowed One.*
> *Patience, then.*

Mary said, "Behold, I am the handmaid of the Lord. May it be done to me according to your word." Then the angel departed from her. (Lk 1:38 NAB)

Mary uses the same word the angel used only a few moments earlier: "behold" (*idou*) (see Lk 1:31). The root word for "behold" carries the meaning "to perceive," "to see," or "to know." The very first action of Mary at the appearance and message of the angel was to see (see Lk 1:29). In the passage, "seeing" deepens progressively. The seeing is a deepening of faith. The word "behold" (*idou*) summons the hearer to pay special attention. With this word the Blessed Mother summons the angel and us to heed the deepening of the mystery that Mary is now poised to utter. Notice the reversal of emphasis: the angel has announced to Mary that she is favored of God and the Lord is with her. Furthermore, the angel has proclaimed that Mary is to conceive and be the Mother of God's only Son, who will save the world from sin. Finally, the angel has announced that to accomplish this motherhood, the power of the Most High will overshadow Mary through the action of the Holy Spirit. Only one thing remains: Our Lady's free consent. God has prepared all else. Nothing is lacking. Salvation history hinges now on the "yes" of the Blessed Virgin Mary. She begins, "Behold" . . . it is she who is the one now making the announcement, proclaiming to the angel and to the world: "Behold I am the handmaid of the Lord. May it be done . . ."

In the very moment when Our Lady utters those words, "May it be done to me . . . ," the word of the angel comes to pass and the ancient promise is fulfilled. The Holy Spirit overshadows her, and the Son of God, without ceasing to be God, takes flesh in her virginal womb. The Word has truly become flesh (see Jn 1:14). Mary's "May it be done to me . . ." is *the moment* at which the incarnation takes place. All the treasures of heaven come to dwell in Mary's womb. Eternity fills time.

> *The cruel axe once wielded cut short the tree of Jesse*
> *The wound in the wood leaves an empty, shorn base*
> *The human family suffers a crude cut—Sin—we are sapped*
>   *of possibility.*

God, leaving no such scar, reaches down
moving freely
to such an impossible place: the womb of the Virgin becomes
sheer fertility.

God has poured himself out . . . so probe then—
Has the axe, with cruel decisiveness, touched your life
leaving a hollowness you fear to enter?
Step with determination; feel along the empty dark
and you'll come upon the One Poured Out
Who overflows the impossible place
and brush close to a stirring most rare:
Hope in motion.

In *Verbum Domini* Benedict XVI notes that the author to the Letter to the Hebrews proclaims:

> Long ago God spoke to our ancestors in many and various ways by the prophets, but in these last days he has spoken to us by a Son, whom he appointed heir of all things, through whom he also created the worlds. He is the reflection of God's glory and the exact imprint of God's very being, and he sustains all things by his powerful word. (Heb 1:1–3)[29]

---

29. See Pope Benedict XVI, *Verbum Domini*, 11.

CHAPTER TWO

The Nativity of Saint John the Baptist

In the days of Herod of Judea, there was a priest named Zechariah, who belonged to the priestly order of Abijah. His wife was a descendant of Aaron, and her name was Elizabeth. Both of them were righteous before God, living blamelessly according to all the commandments and regulations of the Lord. But they had no children, because Elizabeth was barren, and both were getting on in years. Once when he was serving as priest before God and his section was on duty, he was chosen by lot, according to the custom of the priesthood, to enter the sanctuary of the Lord and offer incense. Now at the time of the incense offering, the whole assembly of the people was praying outside. Then there appeared to him an angel of the Lord, standing at the right side of the altar of incense. When Zechariah saw him, he was terrified; and fear overwhelmed him. But the angel said to him, "Do not be afraid, Zechariah, for your prayer has been heard. Your wife Elizabeth will bear you a son, and you will name him John. You will have joy and gladness, and many will rejoice at his birth, for he will be great in the sight of the Lord. He must never drink wine or strong drink; even before his birth he will be filled with the Holy Spirit. He will turn many of the people of Israel to the their God. With the spirit and power of

Elijah he will go before him, to turn the hearts of parents to their children, and the disobedient to the wisdom of the righteous, to make ready a people prepared for the Lord." Zechariah said to the angel, "How will I know that this is so? For I am an old man, and my wife is getting on in years." The angel replied, "I am Gabriel. I stand in the presence of God, and I have been sent to speak to you and to bring you this good news. But now, because you did not believe my words, which will be fulfilled in their time, you will become mute, unable to speak, until the day these things occur."

Meanwhile the people were waiting for Zechariah, and wondered at his delay in the sanctuary. When he did come out, he could not speak to them, and they realized that he had seen a vision in the sanctuary. He kept motioning to them and remained unable to speak. When his time of service was ended, he went to his home. After those days his wife Elizabeth conceived, and for five months she remained in seclusion. She said, "This is what the Lord has done for me when he looked favorably on me and took away the disgrace I have endured among my people." (Lk 1:5–25)

John the Baptist was irreverent from the very beginning. By the secular standard of the time, John even seems to have been regarded as somewhat disrespectful. His neighbors probably agreed that he was at least unpredictable, while some contended he did not know his place. The kinder comments highlighted that perhaps it was simply a case of a young man being too smart for his own good. He stood up publicly and without second thought confronted King Herod, one of the most terrifying leaders of his time: "It is not lawful for you to have your brother's wife" (Mk 6:18; see Mt 14:4). Saint Luke tells us John also spoke out fearlessly against all the evil deeds Herod had committed (see Lk 3:19). John spoke up clearly and told the king himself that he needed to reform his life. John stood up in the face of wrongdoing. He would not remain quiet in the face of falsehood. He spoke out not only against sin but also the illusions with which people surround themselves so as to continue sinning and to avoid conversion.[1] When everyone else feared to speak, John spoke bluntly. He would not settle when others did. He never punted. Herod was at the front of the line of many who wanted to silence John.

Saint John the Baptist did not learn his outspokenness from anyone. He behaved that way from the very start. In fact, shortly after his birth, the first time his parents brought him to the synagogue a heated discussion about his name interrupted the proceedings (see Lk 1:59–65).

And John's tendency to raise his hand or interrupt was contagious. When the angel Gabriel came to announce John's birth to his father Zachariah, the archangel *interrupted* a religious ceremony: "Once when he was serving as priest before God and his section was on duty, he was chosen by lot, according to the custom of the priesthood, to enter the sanctuary of the Lord and offer incense. Now at the time of the incense offering, the whole assembly of the people was praying outside. Then there appeared to him an angel of the Lord, standing at the right side of the altar of incense" (Lk 1:8–11).

That which a good many experts and people in the know said was to be, John predicted would *not be*. In fact, he declared without hesitation it would be *the opposite*. Where others declared "case closed," John customarily and firmly reopened it.

---

1. See Jean Daniélou, *The Work of John the Baptist* (Baltimore: Helicon Press, 1966), 60.

John had a lot to do with opening what had otherwise been declared closed, whether it be a womb, a mouth, or a mind. The best medical opinion of the day declared that Elizabeth his mother was sterile and would never conceive a child. That which others declared closed, John opened. Even more, his father Zachariah failed to trust the word of the angel, and in punishment was made unable to speak (see Lk 1:18–20). It was John the child who reversed the word of no less than an archangel, as Zachariah speaks the moment he writes, "His name is John" (Lk 1:63). John opened what heaven declared closed. And, when he was only nine days old, and the relatives, friends, and neighbors insisted that the custom hold firm: John should be named after his father (see Jn 1:59–63). That which popular opinion professed, his mother and father declared otherwise on John's behalf.

We in our day could stand to be a lot more like John. The way of the world is so often closed. God's way is open. We settle for things far too easily, but John did not settle. John spoke so clearly only because he listened so intently to God. He went into the desert and gladly left behind the noise of the world so as to listen to God's word. Because John spoke up fearlessly, it is ironic that his first gift to his father Zachariah was silence. That silence was more penance than punishment. The new silence imposed by the angel protected Zachariah. It strengthened him, and it was also a sign to his friends and relatives. When they *heard his silence,* they realized Zachariah had seen a vision. His silence spoke more clearly than his words. In one sense, his silence converted him more than the vision of the angel did. John's affection for silence is meant to inspire us as well.

It inspired the anchoresses, religious women who lived as hermits in the thirteenth century. They wrote in the guide for their members that John the Baptist, so favored by God, knew that even the most committed Christians take a great risk when they live amidst the noise, hurry, and crowds of the world.[2] Johannes Tauler, a fourteenth-century German mystical writer, emphasizes that when we speak we prevent God from doing so.[3] God utters his Word in silence.

John's first reported action is the leap or dance he performs in the womb of his mother Elizabeth at the sound of the Virgin Mary's voice. This early action of John is a prophetic witness to the Blessed Mother, to the presence of the Lord Jesus and to the inviolable dignity of the child in the womb. John reveals to us the beauty of the child. Far from being a problem or an inconvenience, the child is by far the answer for the most complex difficulties of our day and the problems of everyday life. The child is the one who lives in the emphatic present, who moves on immediately to the next adventure, even creating one if need be.[4] The child has the widest of eyes and the most daring of spirits. Adrienne von Speyr tells us that the love of the Lord is especially visible to children.[5] She likewise explains that this immediacy is a sense of welcome that pervades the experience of the child and underlies the child's simple confidence.[6] Saint John the Baptist never stopped being a child. He grew *up*, but he never grew *old*. He never lost the identity that was his even from the womb. The child is God's answer, yet so many today refuse God and his answer.

---

2. See Anne Savage and Nicholas Watson, trans., *Anchoritic Spirituality: Ancrene Wisse and Associated Works.* The Classics of Western Spirituality Series (Mahwah, NJ: Paulist Press, 1991), 107.

3. Johannes Tauler, *Sermons.* The Classics of Western Spirituality Series (Mahwah, NJ: Paulist Press, 1985), 38.

4. See Hans Urs von Balthasar, *Unless You Become Like This Child* (San Francisco: Ignatius Press, 1991), 50.

5. See Adrienne von Speyr, *The Letter to the Colossians* (San Francisco: Ignatius Press, 1998), 136.

6. See Adrienne von Speyr, *The Letter to the Ephesians* (San Francisco: Ignatius Press, 1996), 136.

When did you and I stop looking other people in the eye? When did we start to doubt ourselves and worry? When did we begin to navel gaze and start to be depressed? It was, quite simply, when we stopped being children. We move so quickly through the day and through life that we can't spare the time to hold a door for the next person, greet another, or learn someone's name. When did we get so busy? Perhaps it was the first time we were rejected, or when someone told us that we walked funny, or that we did not throw the baseball hard enough. It was then that we averted our eyes. We started to move at the speed of anxiety rather than the confident pace of love. We began to want to fit in and to be popular at all costs. We thought being the smartest, the most stylish, or the most outwardly religious would fix us and make the pain go away. Since then, maybe we tried to put substances into our body that would numb us, or substances on the outside of our body that would somehow make us appear more beautiful or acceptable.

If so, John the Baptist's first message is for us. The child reminds us never to give in to disillusionment or discouragement. Jesus solemnly reminds us: "Truly I tell you, unless you change and become like children, you will never enter the kingdom of heaven" (Mt 18:3). In this the child is the answer to every malady we have: We must become children again, faithful to the child we once were, to that little person who is so mysterious to us now, who even then possessed all of our creativity.[7] In the child each of us finds the answer to the anxiety we face every day. The child knows intuitively that very few anxieties are healed or decreased by our dwelling on them.[8] The child has,

---

7. See John Saward, *The Way of the Lamb: The Spirit of Childhood and the End of the Age* (San Francisco: Ignatius Press, 1999), 99ff.

8. See Adrienne von Speyr, *The World of Prayer* (San Francisco: Ignatius Press, 1985), 180.

and more so *is*, the answer to our fears and preoccupations. We are not the sum of all our mistakes in life. We may make mistakes, but we never *are* a mistake.

Heaven listened to John the Baptist. Heaven listens to the child. We had better listen too. This is the only lasting way to overcome disillusionment and self-centeredness. As Catholics, our reverence for life might seem irreverent to others, or even an imposition on them. But human life is *never* an imposition. Human life cannot get in the way because *it is the way*. Life is the union of love: What is it that makes you and me *ourselves*? How did we become human and receive life? Was it when we could sign a mortgage? Was it when we moved into a college dorm? Was it when we went on our first, second, or third date? No, because people who never do any of those things are *still* people. Was it when we were enrolled in school? Was it when we began to walk? Was it when we could speak or make sounds? No, because some people never do some or any of these things, and they are still human persons. When did we become human? Was it when we were lifted from our mother's womb, or when the doctor cut the umbilical cord? A picture is worth a thousand words: The ultrasound picture of the child in the womb tells us to look sooner. When did we become persons? What was it in my innermost world that constituted me as a separate human life? What was the threshold, the point of no return, beyond which you and I became *our very self*? Is dependency on others a crime, for which we are declared *inhuman*?

The irreplaceable and unchangeable moment of human life is founded on *the two becoming one*. When our father and mother *became one*, in and through their personal gift of self, their gametic donations fused and became one in the body of our mother. We began in that very instant of union, and we will *never end*. Even death cannot fully conquer that moment. Before that moment of union, what our father gave and what our mother gave, taken individually and separately, would never come to sign a mortgage, drive a car, or go on a date. In that moment of union what the two gave became one—became each of us—a separate and independent self. Though helpless and needy, this self directs itself from within while it naturally relies on the mother's body. Prior to that union, *I* did not exist, but after it *I* will never cease to exist. Reliance is not a crime.

The Supreme Court decision *Roe v. Wade* and all of the attacks on the child since then, including human embryonic stem cell research, are blind. We must *treasure*, not harvest or abort, the child in the womb. The child is not a prize or trophy that one has a right to claim; the child is a gift of life and love. John would object, and so should we: *The child in the womb is human life from the very first moment of conception.* No law, no compromise can say otherwise. The battle we face today is not faith versus science, but ethical science versus unethical science.

We must believe in the child, for the child is the one who finds the way for the rest of us. The danger we face today is that as we move so quickly through our daily life, so many people do not treat others in a human way. We are often the first to forget what it is to be human. It takes a child to know what it is to be human. The child is the one who finds the way for us. Yet, in our day we legislates against the child.

Even from the womb, John the Baptist changed the world. He felt the presence of the Messiah in the sound of the voice of the Blessed Mother (see Lk 1:44), and John leapt, or danced, in the womb for joy. Even from the womb, he saw all the way to heaven, and he moved heaven. If the child in the womb can move heaven, then surely, an adult must be able to move the world. Our strength to do so comes from Jesus in the Holy Eucharist: in the presence of the Eucharist John's earliest action becomes our own: we leap for joy.

John interrupts, which is to say he irrupts. He just wouldn't behave or go along to get along—thank God! And we have to do it too. We hold human life sacred, with an inviolable dignity from the first moment of conception to the moment of natural death. We have to be faithful to the child we used to be and, though it may seem irreverent, unmannerly, or perhaps illegal, we go back to the classroom, the office, and the supermarket, and we interrupt so as to be faithful, and speak up for the child.

CHAPTER THREE

Christmas: The Nativity of Our Lord

In those days a decree went out from Emperor Augustus that all the world should be registered. This was the first registration and was taken while Quirinius was governor of Syria. All went to their own towns to be registered. (Lk 2:1–3)

C aesar launches a grand scheme—he wants to start taking names. His ambitious task is to count the total inhabitants of the entire known world. Caesar's ambition is matched only by his pride. He wants to count, to number, all of his subjects. For Caesar, as for any worldly leader, it all adds up: those who seek power also want control. And control must be bolstered at regular intervals. He will count his subjects and then lean back and remind himself how powerful he is. In fact, once he takes the tally, why not *tax* the tally? Caesar is calculating in more ways than one. After all, it is far better to count money than people. More people on the books meant more money for the dictator.

And so the ruler of this world sets to counting by taking down names. Names are important; they mean something. Names indicate unique identity. In the ancient world, to know someone's name meant to be able to summon their spirit. Ordinarily, a lot of thought goes into the name a child will receive at birth. The name "Caesar" refers to the Roman dictator. Dictators like to rule, and they want to be in control. What better way to be in control than by having power over other people? What better way to have power than to record their names on a list? Of course, one who has power must give orders in order to wield that power. Control's central myth is that if we could just somehow change everyone around us, we would be happy. Control is blame's natural follow-through.

In his pride, Caesar wants to affect the entire world. His pride, of course, is only a small measure of the pride of the prince of this world. With all of his power, rules, and orders, Caesar is doing much more than counting the inhabitants of his kingdom or seeking to expand the tax base. On a deeper level, Caesar is *laying down a challenge to God*. Caesar is seeking to number and name the people of God, and in doing so is saying that God's people belong to Caesar. But God's people belong only to God. By attempting to count the people of God, Caesar offends as did King David when he attempted such a numbering (see 2 Sm 24:2–17). The people of God are a multitude that no one can count (see Rev 7:9). The author of the Letter to the Hebrews speaks of those "enrolled in heaven" (Heb 12:23).[1] Caesar's census thus defies the Divine: Caesar

---

1. "But you have come to Mount Zion and to the city of the living God, the heavenly Jerusalem, and to innumerable angels in festal gathering, and to the assembly of the firstborn who are enrolled in heaven, and to God the judge of all, and to the

proclaims that God is limited and God's people leaderless. Ironically, among those whom the imperial counter deemed to number his subjects was the One who created Caesar. In counting the people, Caesar is flexing his control not only against man, but against God.

Worry: The World's Most Common Ponzi Scheme

The tendency to control is not limited to Caesar or to dictators. Control is a common phenomenon. Some measure of organization, predictability, and stability is important in life. Yet, helpful orderliness differs greatly from stifling control. We do have legitimate reasons to consider and take seriously a wide array of our day-to-day responsibilities. Yet often even these genuine concerns bog us down with worry. When we corner ourselves and others with high expectations and demands, we may have drifted from structure to regimentation. Something of Caesar's pride can then seep into our own hearts.

Everyone thought Caesar had it made. He was in control. His word, even his *whim*, was law. Yet, ironically even the ruler is not free. To gain control often means to give up authentic freedom. Notice those who appear on the margins: the shepherds. In Biblical times, the shepherd was most difficult to control. His itinerant, nomadic lifestyle allowed him to appear almost invisible. He was difficult to tax, or, for that matter, to count. In fact, the shepherd was often ranked with thieves and murderers. We become suspicious of what we cannot predict or control. But the angels of the nativity are drawn to the

---

spirits of the righteous made perfect, and to Jesus, the mediator of a new covenant, and to the sprinkled blood that speaks a better word than the blood of Abel" (Heb 12:22–24).

shepherds. Because of their lifestyle and work, shepherds learn early that control is a myth. One cannot control the weather, the sheep, or the land. Instead of controlling the sheep, the shepherd knows he must lead the sheep. Controlling and leading are not synonyms but opposites. Because he knows what it is to lead, the shepherd can follow. The one who is "in control" cannot follow angels, stars, or dreams, but only the same exhausting regimen.

We give in to the temptation to control, even if our lives do not appear rigid. Our house might look very "lived-in." Piles might clutter our desk, and crumbs litter our car. The control that is so painful is not about our outer world but our inner world. Control is not simply about how meticulously we keep our files or calendar. We can just as easily become unbending and unyielding in our relationships. Instead of being predictable, we become inflexible. Over time we can even inadvertently become overly demanding of others and highly critical of them. This is often because we set unrealistic standards of what we have dubbed "success."[2] The fallacy insists that we can only allow ourselves or others to relax when we reach this imagined, self-imposed standard. Since the bar is set so high, no one, including ourselves, ever reaches it. So we can never relax and simply enjoy life. Everything becomes a race. For example, while doing homework well is important, we can unduly pressure our children to meet unrealistic standards, making them repeat assignments until they are flawless. Our expectations of friends and coworkers can grow to such a degree that we misinterpret innocent actions for insults. No one makes the outright decision to be controlling. Control is an attitude that seeps into our lives and blends in with our

---

2. See Simon Tugwell, OP, *Prayer: Living With God* (Springfield, IL: Templegate, 1975), 54.

lifestyle. It seeps in so gradually that we can no longer distinguish between control and daily life.

Where does our tendency to control come from? Control thrives on worry. Our legitimate everyday concerns drift into a kind of torment that disturbs our mind and troubles our heart. While worry is supposed to alleviate problems, many discover that worry *itself* is a problem. It is so difficult to shake because it becomes a way of life. Worry surfaces in almost any circumstance and pushes responsible concern and care into anxiety. Worry disengages us from people to the point that we put all our energy into outcomes. Worry diminishes meaning and underlies the drive to control. The common tendency to worry about and therefore to control our work, school, and family is wired to somehow satisfy our intangible needs and expectations. Worry and control draw and drain an incredible amount of mental energy. Everything we attempt to control we first worry about. Ironically, the tendency to control is so pervasive and intense, yet it often surrounds very mundane and common realities: people attempt to control everything from their finances to the cable channel, from what their boss thinks of them to what their neighbors don't think of them, from their children's grades to the decisions of God himself. For many, worry is standard operating procedure.

Often enough, worry creates a "to-do" list. By its nature, worry *spreads*. Once worry has a lock on one thing in our lives, it attempts to jump into more and more areas until we have a knotted lifestyle of worry and preoccupation. The cycle of worry goes round and round until we may feel as if we can't go on . . . but at the same time we feel we can't give up either. If you tell someone not to worry, they worry all the more. *They worry for having worried.*

Worry is nothing more than an internal Ponzi scheme: it expects too much and brings far too little. Worry is the great fraud, the seemingly acceptable sabotage. It doesn't work, yet most people do it. No one teaches a course or seminar on "worrying more," or "increasing the benefits of worry." Worry gets in the way and blocks our ability to perceive life as it really is.

Worry thrives on self-hate. Self-defeating patterns such as entrenched negative attitudes, the drive for excessive attention, and an extreme focus on the perceived flaws of other people are signs that self-hate may be taking more and more room in our inner life. Self-hate's calling card is perfectionism; its favorite sport is comparing, and its mascot is anger. Self-hate makes us otherwise inaccessible and all but impossible to reach. Self-hate sends our internal dials spinning.

Ultimately, self-hate comes from wounds. Our ultimate wound is sin and fear—fear that we matter so little that nothing will stop someone from rejecting us and hurting us—again. The wounds underlie our tendency to perfectionism, which sends our expectations into orbit, even for routine daily events and experiences. Worry keeps them in orbit. In fact, the frantic rush to meet or attain such towering expectations is itself *another* wound. The vicious cycle continues to spin. Only authentic self-giving love can break the cycle and stop the spinning. We can choose to be like Caesar or like the shepherds. We can choose to count on the world or to follow the innumerable riches of heaven.

> Joseph also went from the town of Nazareth in Galilee to Judea, to the city of David called Bethlehem, because he was descended from the house and family of David. He went to be registered with Mary, to whom he was engaged and who was expecting a child. While they were there, the time came for her to deliver her child. And she gave birth to her first-born son and wrapped him in bands of cloth, and laid him in a manger, because there was no place for them in the inn. (Lk 2:4–7)

"The time came . . ." In the midst of chaotic busyness, of haste and hurry, of the ambitious census of the entire world, something all the more urgent and unstoppable occurs. The census is forever upstaged. Caesar's preparations and plans to count the world in order to demonstrate his own power remain nothing but a feeble attempt. Conversely, Someone all the more powerful emerges in an almost incidental, unhurried, and humble way: Jesus, the Son of God. And for God's Son the world offers "no room." The world has little room for God and even less for the child. Mary and Joseph met a lot of closed doors in Bethlehem that night. Yet, they never allowed the closed doors to become a dead end.

He who was born in Bethlehem longs also to be born in our hearts. Often, our hearts can be as busy as Bethlehem was that night. We may tightly close the doors of our hearts. In trying to make room for so many other things we not only miss, but we *turn away from*, the One who *creates* our hearts.

"The time came . . ." In the rickety shelter of Bethlehem's stable two thousand years ago, in a heavenly moment, time's long corridor of closed doors opened at the intersection of eternity. Time meets and welcomes eternity. It was from and for this moment that time was created. We often mistakenly *reduce time* to the movement of the calendar. Time is larger than its measure. Space now too must make room for the One who rules all time. Time welcomes him, whereas it seems space shrinks and withdraws: He is given the last place. And the last place becomes, miraculously, the first. The Son of God, born of a virgin, born in a stable, is wrapped in swaddling clothes and laid in a manger. He who will multiply the loaves and will give his flesh for real food and his blood for real drink (see Jn 6:55), is laid in a place for feeding, a manger. In fact, the name Bethlehem means "house of bread," because it was a grain-producing area in Old Testament times.

Christmas Night

The destination is enclosed by the timber of a stable
as the endurance of pregnancy gives way.
Newborn arms unfold to welcome a kingly quest:
wise men, shepherds, and angels close their trail today.
yet this child's eyes start a search far more severe;
His mission turns attention beyond the guests humbled,
        bowing near.

He grasps for a splinter of the manger's
beam.
His mother quickly bends and supplies
substituting her finger to satisfy
a Savior's scream.

One day his insistent reach, undeterred will find
the object of his grasp:
a beam far more sure than this stable
which he will muscle well and wield and be death's slay
His thirst-filled cry complete at last.

In that region there were shepherds living in the fields, keeping watch over their flock by night. Then an angel of the Lord stood before them, and the glory of the Lord shone around them, and they were terrified. But the angel said to them, "Do not be afraid; for see—I am bringing you good news of great joy for all the people: to you is born this day in the city of David a Savior, who is the Messiah, the Lord. This will be a sign for you: you will find a child wrapped in bands of cloth and lying in a manger." And suddenly there was with the angel a multitude of the heavenly host, praising God and saying, "Glory to God in the highest heaven, and on earth peace among those whom he favors!" (Lk 2:8–14)

Caesar orders the earthly census. As if in response, God sets forth a census of the heavens as the angels fill the sky at the nativity of Our Lord. If you are going to send an angel to someone, you would think that such a person would be very dignified and deserving of the visit. After all, angels are heavenly beings. To announce the birth of the Lord, the angel appears not to the aristocrat, the noble, or the wealthy. The angel does not even appear in this instance to the overly religious. God and his messengers are attracted to the poor and the lowly, to those who live on the margins, to the forgotten and the outcast. To announce the news of the birth of the Son of God, the angel of the Lord appears to common shepherds. They probably were not known to be overly polite or mannerly. Their standing in society was probably doubtful to say the least. They were earthy and unrefined. After all, the shepherds worked in the fields at night and had to contend with wolves and other predators. Yet, the angels sought out the shepherds for this good news. After the Holy Family and the angels themselves, the shepherds were first to visit the newborn King. The shepherds of that first Christmas were called away from their sheep to the very Lamb of God.

The appearance to the shepherds differs somewhat from that of the annunciation to Our Lady. As the angels appear, the glory of the Lord shines around the shepherds. The angels proclaim the birth of the Lord but do not dialogue with the shepherds. Could it be that angels and shepherds have a lot in common? The shepherd is like an angel for the sheep.

The Son of God's first visitors were those who dwell on the margins. That which comes first tends to go deep and last long. Jesus would frequently use the image of the shepherd in his public ministry. He would even use the image of the Good Shepherd to describe himself. Could it be that this early encounter left an impression on Jesus in some way?

When the angels had left them and gone into heaven, the shepherds said to one another, "Let us go now to Bethlehem and see this thing that has taken place, which the Lord has made known to us." So they went with haste and found Mary and Joseph, and the child lying in the manger. When they saw this, they made known what had been told them about this child; and all who heard it were amazed at what the shepherds told them. But Mary treasured all these words and pondered them in her heart. The shepherds returned, glorifying and praising God for all they had heard and seen, as it had been told them. (Lk 2:15–20)

The shepherds have just seen a vision of angels and heard them signing and praising God. But the shepherds do not comment on or sensationalize this marvel. Instead, they begin a quest. True marvels lead us and rouse us to go forth. It is not the vision of angels that the shepherds proclaim, but the message, and that they "found Mary and Joseph, and the infant lying in the manger." In this, the shepherds become the first evangelists, and in a sense, they become angels insofar as they take on the task of the angels and become messengers: the shepherds now announce what the angels announced to them. And those who hear the shepherds become, in a sense, shepherds themselves, whose amazement leads them to go and see with their own eyes "this thing that has taken place" (Lk 2:15).

CHAPTER FOUR

"Isn't This the Son of Joseph?"

When he came to Nazareth, where he had been brought up, he went to the synagogue on the sabbath day, as was his custom. He stood up to read, and the scroll of the prophet Isaiah was given to him. He unrolled the scroll and found the place where it was written:

> "The Spirit of the LORD is upon me,
> because he has anointed me
> to bring good news to the poor.
> He has sent me to proclaim release to the captives
> and recovery of sight to the blind,
> to let the oppressed go free,
> to proclaim the year of the LORD's favor."

And he rolled up the scroll, gave it back to the attendant, and sat down. The eyes of all in the synagogue were fixed on him. Then he began to say to them, "Today this scripture has been fulfilled in your hearing." All spoke well of him and were amazed at the gracious words that came from his mouth. They said, "Is not this Joseph's son?" He said to them, "Doubtless you will quote to me this proverb, 'Doctor, cure yourself!' And you will say, 'Do here also in your hometown the things that we have heard you did at Capernaum.'" And he said, "Truly I tell you, no prophet is accepted in the prophet's hometown. But the truth is, there were many widows in Israel in the time of Elijah, when the heaven was shut up three years and six months, and there was a severe famine over all the land; yet Elijah was sent to none of them except to a widow at Zarephath in Sidon. There were also many lepers in Israel in the time of the prophet Elisha, and none of them was cleansed except Naaman the Syrian." When they heard this, all in the synagogue were filled with rage. They got up, drove him out of the town, and led him to the brow of the hill on which their town was built, so that they might hurl him off the cliff. But he passed through the midst of them and went on his way. (Lk 4:16–30)

First words are crucial. They set the scene and the direction when a person begins a new venture. You have to hit the right note early.

The first three chapters of Luke's Gospel tell us about the annunciation of Our Lord and his Nativity, the presentation and finding in the temple, the baptism of Jesus and his temptation by the devil. But in the fourth chapter we hear the first words of the *public ministry* of Jesus, which he now begins among the people.

Jesus enters the synagogue, the Scripture tells us, "as was his custom" (Lk 4:16). Throughout his public ministry Jesus regularly entered the synagogue and taught (see Mk 1:39; Mt 4:23; 9:35; Lk 4:44). He knew the synagogue well, its blessings and its prayerful moments. He was also very familiar with how the hypocrites behaved in the synagogue (see Mt 6:2, 5). The solemn practice was to gather in the synagogue to pray and listen to Scripture on every Sabbath and every feast day, a custom

Jesus followed from his early childhood.[1] When he was only twelve years old, the Holy Family went on a pilgrimage to the Temple in Jerusalem. On the way home, the Virgin Mary and Saint Joseph could not find the child Jesus. So they retraced their steps and found him in the temple, his Father's house, talking to the doctors of the law (see Lk 2:42–51). When Jesus seems lost or missing in our lives, when we feel we have lost our way, we should do what Our Lady and Saint Joseph did. They knew well where to find him.

And so Jesus now enters the synagogue and speaks the first words of his public ministry. At first he doesn't touch on any hot topics or promote any ideology. So far so good, *or so it seems.*

After he reads from the words of Isaiah the prophet, Jesus proclaims those first words of his own public ministry: "Today this scripture has been fulfilled in your hearing" (Lk 4:21). The first word of Jesus is "Today." The passage from Isaiah said, "The Spirit of the Lord God is upon me . . . to bring good news to the oppressed, . . . captives, . . . the prisoners" (Is 61:1). In the eyes of God, this is what gives meaning: to go in compassion to the poor, the captive, the blind, and the oppressed . . . *today.* And Jesus, the Son of God, is the One who announces the word of the prophet and invests it with his own authority in a new way. The Son of God takes his word to those who live on the margins, to those whom society has cast aside. But that word . . . "today." Society, and sometimes we ourselves, prefer a different word: tomorrow. Couldn't he have just said "tomorrow"? Tomorrow we will do all of this; tomorrow we will do the good work. Society loves tomorrow. Let us *rest* today. We arrange today so that tomorrow will be perfect and comfortable. The world hates the word "today" because the world is fearful and

---

1. Prosper Grech, *An Outline of New Testament Spirituality*, 54.

anxious for tomorrow. Anger can't see "today" because it is all caught up with yesterday. But the word of Jesus tells us: go forth and offer genuine love *today*.

So far so good. They are amazed at him and his teaching.

Yet, a voice calls out: "Is not this Joseph's son?" (Lk 4:22). They think they remember him. They think they know where he comes from. They want him to be familiar—and the familiar is safe. Some want to remember, but for some it is simply too close to home. He mentioned the poor, the captive, the oppressed—those who live on the margins. If *we* bring *them* close, or go out to *them*, we *move* the margins. And sooner rather than later, we will be on the margins. The margins aren't safe. And neither, it seems, is Jesus. Let's bring him down to size: "Isn't this Joseph's son?" In the Gospel of Saint Matthew, the crowd raises a similar plea: "Is not this the carpenter's son?" (Mt 13:55). Let's try to minimalize and condense him and measure down his message. They want to define the Son of God merely in terms of the world. In a sense they are wrong about Jesus. In fact, Saint Bonaventure says that they attempt to insult Jesus by their words.[2] Jesus is *not* the son, but the *adopted* son of his foster father Saint Joseph. If he was *only* the son of Joseph, we could keep what he said at arm's length, or better yet, hand it over to a board, committee, or task force for extended study.

But, " 'The Spirit of the Lord is upon me' . . . Today this scripture has been fulfilled in your hearing" (Lk 4:18, 21).

He speaks with the authority of the One on whom the Spirit of the Lord rests, and he alone brings fulfillment.[3] Today.

---

2. Saint Bonaventure, "Commentary on the Gospel of Luke" in *Works of Saint Bonaventure,* vol. VIII, part I, ed. Robert J. Karris, OFM (Saint Bonaventure, NY: Franciscan Institute Publications, 2001), 330.

3. See German Bishops' Conference, *The Church's Confession of Faith: A Catholic Catechism for Adults* (San Francisco: Ignatius Press Communio Books, 1987), 184.

If he were *only just* the son of Joseph, we could keep those hard sayings at bay. We could keep the cross at bay. We could put it all off to a distant and safe tomorrow.

If he were only the son of Joseph, his saying could simply be like those of Gandhi or Confucius. His teaching could be simply like that of Plato or Aristotle. If he were just the son of Joseph, he would only be giving advice. Take it or leave it. But he is the *adopted* son of Joseph. Jesus *is* the Son of God. His sayings and teaching are not just a theory, a philosophy, or a movement. The very meaning of the universe, life, and salvation itself hinges on his every word and very breath.

He opens up the Old Testament, unrolls the scroll of the prophet Isaiah and finds the passage that speaks of the Spirit of the Lord (*pneuma kyriou*). In speaking about the Spirit of the Lord, Jesus the Son is speaking of the Holy Spirit. The Second Person of the Blessed Trinity is speaking of the Third Person, coeternal and coequal with the Father and the Son. Even though the people will resist what Jesus says, they cannot help but hear the beauty of his words: "All . . . were amazed at the gracious words that came from his mouth" (Lk 4:22). The gracious words that came from the mouth of the Son are the breath of the Holy Spirit. The Greek word for "came from" is *ekporeuomenois*. This word means "to proceed or flow forth" as if from a river, and it is related to the word *peira*, which means "to know by experience": Jesus is thus pouring forth, by his very words, a manifestation of his own experience of the Holy Spirit.

His words are not simply academic musings or abstract theory but proceed from his very substance, from his relation with his Father in the Holy Spirit. Jesus, the anointed One of God (see Acts 10:38), is the One whom the Father has consecrated and sent into the world—the Christ. He tells the people that this passage from the prophet Isaiah is now fulfilled in their hearing (see Lk 4:21). The Holy Spirit had descended

upon the Lord at his baptism and was with the Lord throughout his public ministry.[4] Saint John tells us that Jesus gave the
Holy Spirit to the apostles on Easter Sunday evening (see Jn
20:22). The fullness of the Holy Spirit was given in a remarkable way on the day of Pentecost (see Acts 2:1–13), after which
those gathered *heard* the apostles speaking in their own language (see Acts 2:6).[5] But now, in the synagogue, Jesus imparts
a sign of the future coming of the Holy Spirit to those
gathered.

His words cause them to *wonder* or *marvel* (*ethaumazon*).
The Greek word can have a similar meaning to our word "enthusiasm." The movement and action of the Holy Spirit, ever so
gently, *enthuses* us.[6] This word is used several times in the
Gospels. People would often wonder at the words and actions
of Jesus. They would wonder when he calmed the sea and the
wind (see Mt 8:27), and when he cured the paralytic (see Mt
9:8). This word is also used to describe the response of Jesus: He
marvels at the faith of the centurion (see Mt 8:10) and at the
unbelief of his own people (see Mk 6:6). Wonderment or marvel at the words and deeds of Jesus is also an invitation to glorify
God: the multitudes marveled when he restored speech (see Mt
9:33), when he made the lame walk and the blind see (see Mt
15:31). Such wonderment is not an end in itself but is meant to
lead *to the glory of God* (see Mt 15:31). The signs of Jesus cause
wonder but are not meant to stop at wonder. The wonder leads
us to glorify God. This same word is used three other times:

---

4. See Prosper Grech, *Acts of the Apostles Explained: A Doctrinal Commentary* (New
York: Alba House, 1966), 29.

5. Ibid., 25.

6. See Hans Urs von Balthasar for the theological sense of this word: *The Glory of the
Lord A Theological Aesthetics I: Seeing the Form* (San Francisco: Ignatius Press, 1989),
123.

when Pilate marvels at the silence of Jesus (see Mk 15:5); when Pilate learns of the death of Jesus on Good Friday (see Mk 15:44); and earlier, when Jesus told the crowd, "Give therefore to the emperor the things that are the emperor's, and to God the things that are God's" (Mt 22:21). Saint Matthew tells us in the very next line, "When they heard this, they were amazed; and they left him and went away" (Mt 22:22). It is as if the words only a few verses earlier are fulfilled: "For many are called, but few are chosen" (Mt 22:14). So too in the synagogue this day: *The people are unwilling to let their wonderment and marvel* lead them to glorify God. They want wonder for wonder's sake. They want the hysteria and excitement but not the cross. When wonder means they'll have to change their lives, they resist.

And then, in the synagogue on this day, Jesus goes one step farther—even, or so they think, one step too far:

> He said to them, "Doubtless you will quote to me this proverb, 'Doctor, cure yourself!' And you will say, 'Do here also in your hometown the things that we have heard you did at Capernaum.'" And he said, "Truly I tell you, no prophet is accepted in the prophet's hometown. But the truth is, there were many widows in Israel in the time of Elijah, when the heaven was shut up three years and six months, and there was a severe famine over all the land; yet Elijah was sent to none of them except to a widow at Zarephath in Sidon. There were also many lepers in Israel in the time of the prophet Elisha, and none of them was cleansed except Naaman the Syrian." (Lk 4:23–27)

So much for setting. So much for script.

They want him to do for them all of the great deeds they had heard so much about: multiply loaves, turn water into wine, cure the sick here *first*. Be our caterer and fix all that we need— and then we will believe in you. Wonder for wonder's sake. And Jesus, the One on whom the Spirit of the Lord rests, the Son of

God, says that we must go not simply to the widow but to the *foreign* widow. We must embrace not simply the captive but the *foreign* captive; not just the leper but the leper from the *foreign land who might not speak our language.*

Suddenly, the people who only a moment ago were filled with enthusiasm and wonder are now "filled with fury." Wrath replaces enthusiasm. They turn away from glorifying God and turn to anger and rejection. Jesus, it seems, has gone not to the hot topic—but to the *hotter* topic.

The people get angry. The crowd is leaning over whispering to one another, pointing toward Jesus, their brows furrowed and deeply creased like the curve of that hill they have in mind.

He means it. Not just the poor, the captive, and the oppressed, but the *foreigner* who is poor, the *stranger* who is captive, and the *immigrant* who is oppressed.

Now the veins in their foreheads are popping. Eyebrows raise while eyes roll. Contempt flows. He has told them that they have to smash the mirrors. He has told them that God does not conform to their ways. He has confronted them with their own all but impenetrable self-centeredness. He tells them to go to the margins. This is the momentum of Christianity that so many would like to slow down or hand off to someone else. We have to step into the margins. That is where Christianity *lives.* We have to step onto the margins and, for example, call the person we have not talked to in three years. We have to step onto the margins and cry out that immigrants be welcomed in the name of the Son of God who fled into Egypt as a refugee at the fury of the tyrant Herod. We have to step onto the margins and point out that cohabitation, adultery, and contraception are lies that always hurt the person. We have to proclaim that the same fury of Herod that murdered the Holy Innocents is now unleashed on the world in procured abortion, and that human beings, let alone Catholics, can in no way, shape, or form support abortion. As Blessed Pope John Paul II taught, the right to life is the first of the fundamental rights.[7] We must step onto the margins and go to the lost place and *love*, because love grows bold at the margins. And love loves to break bonds.

Their response?

> . . . all in the synagogue were filled with rage. They got up, drove him out of the town, and led him to the brow of the hill on which their town was built, so that they might hurl him off the cliff. (Lk 4:28–29)

The people of that town have found Jesus, like Our Lady and Saint Joseph found him so many years ago, but completely unlike them, the people are unwilling to accept words of Jesus. They reject him they drive the adult Jesus *out* of the synagogue in Nazareth. The One whom they ought to follow they now lead to the brow of a hill. In fact, their response is worse than that of the devil. In tempting Our Lord, the devil urged him to *throw himself* down from the parapet of the temple (see Lk 4:9). Satan didn't dare *touch* the Lord. But those in the crowd want to throw him over a cliff.

"But he passed through the midst of them and went on his way" (Lk 4:30). Why did Jesus walk away? Saint John tells us elsewhere, "no one laid hands on him, because his hour had not yet come" (Jn 7:30). He walked away because the brow of that hill simply was not high enough. It was not the fitting place;[8] this was, in a poetic sense, not the height from which he would choose to plunge downward into the darkest and most painful place in all of existence. Surely, the Son of God is all sufficient for our salvation, and he needs nothing else. But he wanted to seek out a different hill. He would walk

---

7. See Blessed Pope John Paul II, *Evangelium Vitae*, 20.
8. See Lk 24:26–27, 44–45; *CCC*, no. 572.

from *this* hill to *another*, the hill of Calvary, and through his sacred passion and crucifixion the Son of God gathered the momentum of his sacrifice and broke asunder the gates of hell. And he rose again on the third day.

And today?

Today he has gone to search for the poor, the captive, and the oppressed—whether foreign and domestic, from all times and places. He has gone to search for any and for all of them, for each and for every one of them, for you and for me. He searches them out from Calvary, and he loves them. On Calvary he will repeat that first word he used to begin his public ministry: *today*. And he will repeat it to the heart of a dying thief. "Today you will be with me in paradise" (Lk 23:43). It is as if he is saying, "Today, I am in the darkness with you . . . and my light is stronger than the darkness." As the psalmist says, "O that today you would listen to his voice! Do not harden your hearts" (Ps 95:7–8).

Just as surely as he spoke those words to the people in the synagogue and to the thief on Calvary, he speaks them to us in the Eucharist—*today*.[9]

---

9. See *CCC*, nos. 2605, 2659, 2660.

CHAPTER FIVE

Casting Out a Demon

They went to Capernaum; and when the sabbath came, he entered the synagogue and taught. They were astounded at his teaching, for he taught them as one having authority, and not as the scribes. Just then there was in their synagogue a man with an unclean spirit, and he cried out, "What have you to do with us, Jesus of Nazareth? Have you come to destroy us? I know who you are, the Holy One of God." But Jesus rebuked him, saying, "Be silent, and come out of him!" And the unclean spirit, convulsing him and crying with a loud voice, came out of him. They were all amazed, and they kept on asking one another, "What is this? A new teaching—with authority! He commands even the unclean spirits, and they obey him." At once his fame began to spread throughout the surrounding region of Galilee. (Mk 1:21–28)

It always takes a lot to impress the regulars, the people who show up week after week. Jesus enters the synagogue on the Sabbath and begins to teach. And before him are the regulars, those who came every Sabbath. They have heard many teachers and listened to many lessons. They have seen the best come and go. Some of those attending on that day may have come simply to observe the Law. Perhaps others attended because their parents "said they had to." Still others may have come out of habit or because they were looking for something more. But, they find something different today. They hear a new rabbi speaking, one with a clearer, louder voice. They notice something about his *voice*, about his *words*. People sit up straighter. As they lean forward, they shift and strain in their seats for a better view. Who *is* this? They were "astonished at his teaching, for he taught them as one having authority, and not as the scribes" (Mk 1:22).

Oddly enough, the Gospel passage does not tell us *what Jesus actually said* that astonished them so much. Jesus simply came to Capernaum, and on the Sabbath entered the synagogue and taught. Immediately the people compare his teaching to that of the scribes. Jesus is far better. Why? Did he have the customary three points? Did he use a story to illustrate his main point? The Gospel tells us that the people are astonished because Jesus teaches as one having "authority." In fact, the people refer to this *authority* twice in the passage (see Mk 1:22, 27). Saint Luke also emphasizes the twofold amazement of those who heard Jesus: "They were astounded at his teaching, because he spoke with authority. They were all amazed and kept saying to one another, "What kind of utterance is this? For with authority and power he commands the unclean spirits, and out they come!" (Lk 4:32, 36).

In today's world, "authority" seems to be a bad word, heavy and constraining. Difficulties with authority can easily strain personal and professional relationships. From the earliest age, we have a built-in distain for rules, control, and coercion. We want our own way, not someone else's. Authority triggers the knee-jerk reaction: "I want to have-the-last-word." To the young, "author-ity" sounds like a lame excuse when no other reason will do: "because I said so." Authority is a turnoff in today's world.

But people sense something *different* about the authority of Jesus: it does not repel. It *attracts*. Why?

The Gospel points out that in the midst of Jesus's teaching in the synagogue there was "a man with an unclean spirit, and he cried out, 'What have you to do with us, Jesus of Nazareth? Have you come to destroy us? I know who you are, the Holy One of God'" (Mk 1:23–24). Notice first that the unclean spirit is *in* the synagogue, the holy place. We must use discernment very wisely, for Satan disguises himself as an angel of light (see 2 Cor 11:14). He uses illusion and lies to tempt us. The devil can wreak his influence even in places that are supposed to be good.

The unclean spirit knows the identity of Jesus, but immediately "Jesus rebuked him, saying, "Be silent!'" (Mk 1:25). Jesus first commands the unclean spirit to be quiet to show us that sacred silence is the first response to temptation, to every opening line the devil may use on us. Jesus does not permit the demon to speak because the Lord knows that the demon is a liar (see Jn 8:44). The devil will always mix lies with the truth. Then, the Lord commands: "Come out of him!" (Mk 1:25).

The Gospel tells us, "And the unclean spirit, convulsing him and crying with a loud voice, came out of him" (Mk 1:26). Even though it eventually obeys the Lord's command, the unclean spirit *disobeys* twice. First, it causes a mysterious convulsion. This is not the type of convulsion we might be familiar with, such as one caused by an illness. The passage describes a very different type of convulsion, one induced by the unclean spirit, one that is the *opposite* of *authority* and of *obedience*. As such it is an act of disobedience, not only against God but also against the possessed man. The convulsion is not the type familiar to us and explainable by a physical condition. Rather, it is a sign of the demon disobedient to the will of God and man. The unclean spirit operates in disobedience. It disobeys by taking up residency in the person in the first place, and then by uttering a loud cry to defy the Lord's command: "Be silent!" (Mk 1:25). Finally, the authority of Jesus restores obedience.

Again, the people are astounded: "They were all amazed, and they kept on asking one another, 'What is this? A new teaching—with authority! He commands even the unclean spirits, and they obey him'" (Mk 1: 27). Their astonishment is also a witness: each time Jesus casts out a demon, the evangelist is emphasizing the final victory of Christ over Satan.[1]

The people recognize an authority in Jesus that they are drawn to and acclaim. What happened to authority being an unpopular imposed burden? The Greek word used in the passage for "authority" may hold a clue: *exousia*. Used forty-four times throughout the Gospels to refer to the authority of Jesus, *exousia* comes from the preposition *ek*, meaning "out of," and *ousia*, meaning "substance." The word literally means "out of the substance" or "from the substance." As used in Scripture, *exousia* means authority that comes from the very *substance* of the *person*. Thus, the authority of Jesus flows forth from his very substance. There is no shadow or pretense between who he is and what he says. His words and actions are directly linked to his very substance. Authority or power in the sense of *exousia* is never arbitrary or reactive, but proceeds from the fullness of being and identity in which it inheres. This authority is not based on arbitrary or whimsical influence, well-honed leadership skills, or a "because I can" controlling attitude. Instead, as Balthasar points out, *exousia* means "fullness of power."[2]

---

1. Proper Grech, *An Outline of New Testament Spirituality*, 9.

2. Hans Urs von Balthasar, *The Glory of the Lord: A Theological Aesthetics*. Vol. 1: *Seeing the Form* (San Francisco: Ignatius Press, 1989), 664.

Exousia hints at the nature of the authority of Jesus, why it differs from that of the scribes, and why the people, not to mention the unclean spirits, respond to the word of Jesus. The people recognize that Jesus not only teaches with authority, but that his authority also extends far into the spiritual realm. In the Gospel of Saint John, only one person claims *to have* power or *exousia*: the Roman governor, Pontius Pilate. "So Pilate said to him, "Do you refuse to speak to me? Do you not know that I have power (*exousia*) to release you and I have power (*exousia*) to crucify you?" (Jn 19:10). And the Lord Jesus, who speaks very little during his passion, quickly corrects Pilate: "You would have no power over me unless it had been given you from above" (Jn 19:11). The true nature of *exousia*, its inner secret, is that it is always something given and received. If it is not—if, like Pilate, we claim to possess our own power or authority—then power eludes us. Power turns on the one who seeks to control it. The key with power is: that which is received as a gift can only be exercised as a gift.

This nature of authority as a *gift*, as something *given*, is crucial. Luke's Gospel tells us that Jesus "called the twelve together and gave them power and authority (*exousia*) over all demons and to cure diseases" (Lk 9:1; Mt 10:1). Soon after that, Jesus proclaims, "See, I have given you authority (*exousia*) to tread on snakes and scorpions, and over all the power of the enemy; and nothing will hurt you" (Lk 10:19). *Exousia*, the fullness of power that belongs to Jesus, which he shares with the Twelve, is a reality that is *given* to them by the Lord. Power, *exousia*, can only be *given* and *received*, it can never be *taken* or *possessed*. Balthasar points out that Jesus claims an "*exousia* . . . which he sovereignly communicates as his own to his followers and which, according to his listeners, is the power with which he speaks (see Mk 1:22, 27; 7:29; Lk 4:32, 36)."[3] Just prior to his ascension, Jesus

---

3. Ibid., 472.

confirms that it is of the essence and nature of power that it *can only be received*: "And Jesus came and said to them, 'All authority (*exousia*) in heaven and on earth has been given to me'" (Mt 28:18).

The question for us is: Do we exercise power in the knee-jerk reactive way of the world or in the way of Jesus? Do we exercise power as Pilate does, by seeing it as something we must have? Or do we exercise it as Jesus does: as that which is received and comes forth as a gift from our very substance?

Chapter Six

Follow Me:
The Call of Saint Matthew

As Jesus passed on from there, he saw a man named Matthew sitting at the customs post. He said to him, "Follow me." And he got up and followed him. While he was at table in his house, many tax collectors and sinners came and sat with Jesus and his disciples. The Pharisees saw this and said to his disciples, "Why does your teacher eat with tax collectors and sinners?" He heard this and said, "Those who are well do not need a physician, but the sick do. Go and learn the meaning of the words, I desire mercy, not sacrifice. I did not come to call the righteous but sinners." (Mt 9:9–13, NAB)

The tax collector's table was a cross for a lot of people—except for Matthew. He sat on the other side of the table, collecting the taxes. If someone couldn't pay, the muscle of the military backed up Matthew. Not only that, but Matthew backed up Matthew. The tax code was simple: his job was to collect the tax. Once the government took its share, Matthew could raise the tax a bit more and pocket the difference (see Lk 3:13). So he helped himself, and it got easier every time. And the taxpayers, who knew about the crooked math and funny numbers, couldn't argue. Not in the face of the muscle. Failure to pay meant a higher tax next time, a penalty, prison—or worse. The threat loomed large.

Matthew is not only the one the others pay, but the one they *fear*. So he is unpopular with the tax-paying crowd. But another crowd knows Matthew: the many who the Gospel tells us would go to his house for parties. This crowd enjoys special exemption. They do not pay with money but with their company. They compensate for Matthew's unpopularity. They are friends with Matthew, and as long as they get tax breaks and parties, they keep coming. It doesn't hurt to know Matthew. As a tax collector, he is wealthy. Extortion, then, as now, paid well. The table at Matthew's house, like his tax table, was always well stocked and set, just like his life. Or so he thought.

> As Jesus passed on from there, he saw a man named Matthew sitting at the customs post. (Mt 9:9)

So far, it has been an ordinary workday at the customs post and table. Over the years the shadow of many people fell over his table. They all came, young and old, healthy and sick, wealthy and poor. They had one thing in common: they always walked away poorer, while Matthew walked away richer. He dismissed their excuses and took their money. Not that Matthew ever really noticed any of them, for he had other things on his mind. People were numbers, and the numbers fit in well-defined columns. Matthew's ledger had many columns to be filled in, debts to settle, and money to be made. And where money takes over, there is little room for anything—or anyone—else.

But today, a new shadow falls over Matthew's tax table. Another account is about to come due.

As Jesus passed on from there . . . (Mt 9:9)

How dare he? Pass on? Others stop at the table. They line up, and, more importantly, they pay up. But Jesus passes on. That may be why Matthew noticed him. Jesus stepped out of line. He went in a new direction. He passed on.

Consider the contrast. Jesus is on the move while Matthew sits still. It is as if the new movement of Jesus and the old stubbornness of Matthew collide, sparking new life. Jesus is near, but the moment will not last long. The Lord moves in slow motion, the din of the crowd fades away. Time itself begins to watch.

The tables are about to turn.

As Jesus passed on from there, he saw a man named Matthew sitting at the customs post. (Mt 9:9)

And in this prolonged moment, something *happens*. Jesus *sees* Matthew and says, "Follow me" (Mt 9:9). From Matthew's immediate response—"And he got up and followed him" (Mt 9:9)—it is clear that Matthew also *saw* Jesus. And in this mutual seeing something *occurs*. Something instantaneous takes place. Matthew totters on the brink of death-life. In this moment Matthew has a personal experience of God and sees that only in Jesus can Matthew accomplish all that God asks of him. In this daily moment he sees his life in its real context. The call is the free initiative of God's grace that illuminates Matthew's entire and total existence. Matthew makes an act of faith in response to the word of Jesus.[1] Saint Paul tells us,

---

1. See International Theological Commission, *Theology Today: Perspectives, Principles and Criteria* (Rome: Libreria Editrice Vaticana, 2012), 2.

"So faith comes from what is heard, and what is heard comes through the word of Christ" (Rom 10:17). The act of living faith is not a narrow, robotlike automatic response as if Matthew's freedom is overridden, replaced, or destroyed. Quite the contrary, the look of Jesus enters Matthew's heart, past all of its history, pain, and sin, and pierces it to the core. He has "shone in our hearts" (2 Cor 4:6).

Saint Theresa Benedicta of the Cross explains that at certain moments in our life, through God's action we perceive through supernatural light a spiritual vision that is "much sharper and far clearer than corporeal vision. It is like the sudden illumination by a bolt of lightning, that in a dark night allows things to stand out clear and distinct for a moment. Under the influence of the spiritual light, the objects seen are impressed so deeply on the soul that every time she adverts to them by the grace of God, she beholds them as she did the first time."[2] The experience of God reveals a truth, which Matthew begins to adhere to with his entire person.

In the light of Jesus, the money spread on the table is now worthless. Saint John tells us: "And we know that the Son of God has come and has given us understanding so that we may know him who is true" (1 Jn 5:20). Matthew has *seen* something, recognized *Someone*. And in this Someone, Matthew has seen a glimpse of something that he recognizes but cannot fully describe: the steadfast fidelity of Jesus, who will "lay down his life" (see 1 Jn 3:16). That is how Matthew comes to know love. In his encounter with Jesus, the radiance of the Lord's light penetrates Matthew's heart, opening it to deep love. At the same time, Matthew's response is born of a genuine interior movement, the beginning of a knowledge that is

---

2. Saint Theresa Benedicta of the Cross, *The Science of the Cross* (Washington, DC: ICS Publications, 2002), 72.

as intimate as it is obedient and free. He has found utmost credibility in Jesus. All Matthew can do is surrender in complete freedom, and enter.

The look of Jesus did something *in* the heart of Matthew. Something about that look of Jesus *on* Matthew reaches beyond his deepest wounds, struggles, and conflicts—and finds his original freedom. No one had ever looked at Matthew like this: not those who curse him as they pay the tax, not the strong-arms who back him up, not the hangers-on who tag along for the party. No one. This is the genuine look from the triune depths of God himself. If Matthew had but looked once into the eyes of the poor he took advantage of, he would have seen there the reflection of this radiant light from the eyes of the Lord. Ordinarily Matthew focused on his ledgers and didn't glance at people. Until today. Someone cut into the line today. And Matthew glanced up, away from his ledgers.

No amount of money has weighed this much or meant this much to him. None. *He cannot remember eyes like this*— eyes that see so deeply into him. The look of Jesus sees past all his misdeeds, greed, and guilt. That look of Jesus gives shape to Matthew's very existence. The tables are turning. The words of the psalmist spontaneously become Matthew's own: "Turn to me and be gracious to me . . . (Ps 25:16). The tax table is still in front of Matthew, but it might as well be miles away. Its contents no longer add up to anything. He is already called. He is rejuvenated, made young again, by the act of living faith. In this initial moment he cannot wholly comprehend this call, which has reached into and prevailed in his very depths. His life begins to unfold anew. Matthew rises, steps away from the tax table, and entrusts himself to the persistent fidelity of Christ.

God always moves first. Even the "passing by" of Jesus is not incidental. It has been planned in freedom from all eternity.

When Jesus passes by, his passing by creates a momentum —like the breath and breeze of the Holy Spirit over the chaotic original waters, like the dove from the ark of Noah, like the arms of Moses over the Red Sea—as the Son of God moves over the chaos of Matthew. When this breeze blows past Matthew, caught in its fresh wake, he looks up from the table, up from the chaos, up at Jesus.

Jesus saw him (see Mt 9:9, NAB). God's generous action always precedes our own free action. And the action of God can reach anywhere.

Matthew is used to calling people to account. But now comes a great reversal: "Follow me" (Mt 9:9, NAB). The Gospel tells us that Matthew "got up and followed him" (Mt 9:9, NAB). He leaves the tax table that used to be the cornerstone of his commerce. Now Matthew, like Jesus, is moving. Now Matthew, like Jesus, "passes by." Those in line seize their opportunity. With Matthew's back turned, they slip away. They mark their accounts "paid in full." The backup muscle, too, seize their chance and help themselves to the scattered coins.

The look of Jesus and his word have summoned Matthew, the real Matthew, who is now forever changed. He walks away from the money, which is to say, in terms of Christian discipleship, he walks away *richer*. While this is true for all Christians, it is especially true of priests: Saint Jerome said, "it is the shame of priests if they amass private fortunes . . . A clergyman who engages in business, and who rises from poverty to wealth, and from obscurity to a high position, avoid as you would the plague."[3] Saint Bernard agrees, "As members of that head, crowned with thorns, we should be ashamed to live in luxury;

---

3. Saint Jerome, Letter 52 to Nepotian, 5.

his purple robes are a mockery rather than an honor."[4] Adrienne von Speyr notes, "It is certainly clear as well that wherever external goods and riches are found, Satan is always nearby."[5] Bernanos says there is only one person who can commit the crime of deicide, that is, to kill God in people's hearts. This person is the opulent priest.[6] The Desert Fathers used to say of the priest who asks for money, flee him like the devil. For Matthew, everything that used to make sense is now empty, and everything that before seemed worthless is now rich with meaning and makes sense, anew, in God.

Matthew follows Jesus, who leads the way. But, ironically, Matthew follows Jesus *to Matthew's own house*: "And as he sat at dinner in the house . . ." (Mt 9:10). He who is the Way, *knows the way*. Nothing is hidden from him. And the way forms a procession: "many tax collectors and sinners came" (Mt 9:10). Perhaps they came because it was the usual time for the party with their wealthy friend. Perhaps they came because no one else would have them. And now, Jesus and Matthew sit with them at table. Again, the action of Jesus is always first: "And as he sat at dinner in the house, many tax collectors and sinners came and were sitting with him and his disciples" (Mt 9:10). Before, only Matthew sat at the tax table. He was in control, or so he thought. Now, with Jesus, all sit at the table in Matthew's house. The look and the call of Jesus bring unity. Jesus not only calls Matthew but sits with him. Jesus not only calls us, he also

---

4. Saint Bernard, Abbot, Sermon 2, "Opera Omnia", Edit Cister. 5, 1968, 364–368 in *The Liturgy of the Hours, vol. IV, Office of Readings, Solemnity of All Saints,* (Catholic Book Publishing Co., New York, 1975), p. 1527..

5. Adrienne von Speyr, *Job* (Freiburg, Germany: Johannes Verlag Einsiedeln, 1972), 10. The author is grateful to Msgr. Ronny Jenkins for this translation.

6. See Georges Bernanos "Sermon of an Agnostic on the Feast of Saint Thérèse" in *The Heroic Face of Innocence: Three Stories by Georges Bernanos* (Grand Rapids, MI: Wm. B. Eerdmans Publishing Company, 1999), 27.

sits with us. Mysteriously, the passage does not tell us what Jesus said on that occasion. We don't know if he told a parable. We don't know if he gave them an early rendition of the Beatitudes. But we do know that the same Jesus who looked at Matthew looked at those tax collectors and sinners. And, in this genuine and generous moment, they saw what Matthew saw. Words were not needed for the One Who is the Word.

The Gospel does tell us, however, that another group was there: the Pharisees, who choose not to see what Matthew, the tax collectors, and the sinners see:[7] "When the Pharisees saw this, they said to his disciples, 'Why does your teacher eat with tax collectors and sinners?'" (Mt 9:11). Notice the irony in those words: "The Pharisees saw this . . ." They are the only ones present *who cannot see* what is really going on. But where did the Pharisees come from? How did they suddenly arrive at Matthew's house?

Perhaps a deeper irony is at work: they have followed Jesus. To spy on another, one must follow that other. Even the Pharisees are drawn by the radiant beauty in the words of Jesus to Matthew, "Follow me." But their will resists the light and so they see only the surface. In their pride, they cannot detect the larger movement of the Son of God. Pride blinds. The Pharisees do not in fact see. Instead, *they take notice*.[8] The Pharisees notice Jesus at Matthew's table, eating with tax collectors and sinners. And taking notice the Pharisees serve notice, but not on Jesus directly. Pride gossips: "Why does your teacher eat with tax collectors and sinners?" Whereas Jesus invited Matthew from his tax table, the Pharisees insult Jesus at this table.

7. See *CCC*, no. 588.

8. See Adrienne von Speyr, *Mark: Meditations on the Gospel of Mark* (San Francisco: Ignatius Press, 2012), 101, 108.

This second part of the parable is the first part in reverse. The tables are turning. Not only does pride blind people and incite them to gossip, it also makes them afraid. And fear insults. Because the Pharisees fear Jesus, they do not speak to him directly but to the disciples. That is why they spy on him in the first place. Fear seeks to control: "If you dare step out of line we will talk about you behind your back. If you dare risk real love, we will deliver hate and contempt."

Jesus dares to risk. He has dared Matthew to follow him and dared to sit at table with sinners. Now, he dares again: "Go and learn what this means, 'I desire mercy, not sacrifice'" (Mt 9:12). As Matthew follows, so the Pharisees must go. The tables have turned: for those on the right and those on the left, for the wheat and the chaff, the sick and the well.

"Those who are well have no need of a physician, but those who are sick" (Mt 9:12). Jesus does not diagnose the Pharisees as being "well." He is with the well as friend, brother, and Lord. But he is with the sick as physician, so that they might become friend, brother, and sister, and "hear the word of God and keep it."

The meal in Matthew's house is a rehearsal dinner for something more. Jesus would lead Matthew even farther, to another table in the Upper Room, at the Last Supper. There Jesus would sit again. And, lifting the one bread and one cup, he would turn the tables not just on the Pharisee in all of us but on sin and death itself.

The call of God in our life is a lesson in the unexpected. After all, being God, it is his prerogative to surprise us. For example, God often chooses the unlikely person. When looking for a king to replace Saul, God didn't choose the strong, robust older sons of Jesse. No. God chose Jesse's youngest son, David, a shepherd who played the harp. Jesus, the Son of God, did not choose the best orators, the most highly educated, or the most convincing speakers to announce his Kingdom. Rather, Jesus chose fisherman and tax collectors to proclaim his message. God calls us. His plans are often different from our own.

The call of Saint Matthew seems very direct and immediate. Certainly, he would have his painful moments and times of trial. The summons of the Lord often involves struggle and testing, making the path arduous and grueling. The light of the Lord shines through the darkest of storms and the densest of struggles. Cardinal Charles Journet points out that the light that shone directly on the apostles such as Saint Matthew, also fell on the prophets in the Old Testament.[9] In fact, Jesus compares himself explicitly with Jonah: "For just as Jonah was three days and three nights in the belly of the sea monster, so for three days and three nights the Son of Man will be in the heart of the earth" (Mt 12:40). The story of the prophet Jonah can help us to understand better the way God's call can work in our lives, including the turbulence it may bring.

> Now the word of the LORD came to Jonah son of Amittai, saying, "Go at once to Nineveh, that great city, and cry out against it; for their wickedness has come up before me." But Jonah set out to flee to Tarshish from the presence of the LORD. He went down to Joppa and found a ship going to Tarshish; so he paid his fare and went on board, to go with them to Tarshish, away from the presence of the LORD.
>
> But the LORD hurled a great wind upon the sea, and such a mighty storm came upon the sea that the ship threatened to break up. Then the mariners were afraid, and each cried to his god. They threw the cargo that was in the ship into the sea, to lighten it for them. Jonah, meanwhile, had gone down into the hold of the ship and had lain down, and was fast asleep. The captain came and said to him, "What are you doing sound asleep? Get up, call on your god!

---

9. See Cardinal Charles Journet, *What Is Dogma?* (San Francisco: Ignatius Press, 2011), 26.

Perhaps the god will spare us a thought so that we do not perish." (Jon 1:1–6)

The sailors said to one another: "Come, let us cast lots, so that we may know on whose account this calamity has come upon us." So they cast lots, and the lot fell on Jonah. Then they said to him, "Tell us why this calamity has come upon us. What is your occupation? Where do you come from? What is your country? And of what people are you?" "I am a Hebrew," he replied. "I worship the LORD, the God of heaven, who made the sea and the dry land." (Jon 1:7–9)

Then the men were even more afraid, and said to him, "What is this that you have done!" For the men knew that he was fleeing from the presence of the LORD, because he had told them so. Then they said to him, "What shall we do to you, that the sea may quiet down for us?" For the sea was growing more and more tempestuous. He said to them, "Pick me up and throw me into the sea; then the sea will quiet down for you; for I know it is because of me that this great storm has come upon you." (Jon 1:10–12)

Nevertheless the men rowed hard to bring the ship back to land, but they could not, for the sea grew more and more stormy against them. Then they cried out to the LORD, "Please, O LORD, we pray, do not let us perish on account of this man's life. Do not make us guilty of innocent blood; for you, O LORD, have done as it pleased you." So they picked Jonah up and threw him into the sea; and the sea ceased from its raging. Then the men feared the LORD even more, and they offered a sacrifice to the LORD and made vows. (Jon 1:13–16)

Most likely Jonah had other plans. Prophets often do. No one sets out to be a prophet. No university offers courses on how to be a prophet. You can't register online or get on-the-job training to be a prophet. Only the word of God is needed, along with being in the wrong place at the wrong time. The same is true of finding a prophet. You can't find one; the prophet finds you.

Prophets are the measure and compass of reality, having one foot in eternity and the other in time. They span two worlds at once. They measure and *proclaim* the distance between what is and what ought to be. They take the reading of the awful *already, not yet*. Since prophets exist most readily between two worlds, with a foot firmly planted in both, you cannot nail them down. That is why, in the end, they are most likely to be crucified, literally or figuratively—or both.

Prophets don't simply seek to draw together the two worlds, that of eternity and that of time. No. They seek to draw one world *into the other*, to draw time into eternity. Normally most systems and societies simply cannot *afford* prophets, for they simply cost too much. Prophets are not satisfied with tweaking things. They must *change* them.

At first, however, Jonah, the man who was to be God's prophet, did not want to change a thing. Jonah was minding his own business, not bothering anyone. And one day, God spoke to him. Scripture tells us, "Now the word of the LORD came to Jonah" (Jon 1:1). God's word came to Jonah and asked him to speak up. God asked Jonah to walk right into the center of wickedness and evil and to speak up, to preach against the sin and injustice. We can almost see Jonah's eyebrows rise and disappear into his hairline: "You want me to say *what to whom*?" Run for your life.

Jonah flees from God and from his word: "But Jonah set out to flee to Tarshish from the presence of the LORD" (Jon 1:3). Tarshish is in the far west, which represents the sunset, the dying of the light. It represents darkness and sin. Still, Jonah runs not so much because of sin, but because of fear—the fear that exists at the very brink of love. Such fear is not neurotic fear or the chronic anxiety of worldly fear. The fear that thrives at the margin of love is the fear that knows that if it takes another step toward the beloved there is no turning back. This is fear of the LORD. The prophet's first missionary journey is to himself, for he knows instinctively that if God will chase him that far, God will love him even farther. In running, Jonah is like the child playing outside. When his father tells him it is time to come inside, the child resists. When the father goes to pick him up and carry him inside, the child runs and begins to cry. When the father starts to chase after him the child, unexpectedly, begins to laugh. What was a moment ago a fearful prospect has been transformed, by the chase, into a game. And the child's laugh further transforms the father's pursuit from exasperation into joy. Similarly, only the pursuit of God enables the prophet to go on. Literally then, run for your life.

So Jonah flees. The passage notes he "set out to flee . . . the presence of the LORD" (Jon 1:3). God was with him, and Jonah went away from God. The chase is on. Jonah goes to Joppa and "found a ship going to Tarshish" (Jon 1:3). He "paid his fare" (Jon 1:3) and again we find those terrible words: he "went on board . . . away from the presence of the LORD" (Jon 1:3). When he pays the fare, he is engaging in the ways of the world. He gives in to the marketplace, trading in the goods of the world. He hopes that money will save him from God, for money is power.

God even enlists nature in the pursuit: But the LORD hurled a great wind upon the sea, and such a mighty storm came upon the sea that the ship threatened to break up" (Jon 1:4).[10]

It is as if we have returned to the beginning of Genesis, to the moment of creation itself: "In the beginning when God created the heavens and the earth, the earth was a formless void

---

10. See Paul Murry, OP, *A Journey with Jonah: The Spirituality of Bewilderment* (Dublin: The Columba Press, 2002), 19.

and darkness covered the face of the deep, while a wind from God swept over the face of the waters" (Gn 1:1–2).

After sin, what we think is chaos is really God creating. Now, as then, God hurled the great wind upon the waters. The Holy Spirit hovers over the flight of Jonah. When we resist God, his creativity looks like chaos to our eyes. The storm of God is so great that the very ship on which Jonah flees "threatened to break up" (Jon 1:4). No human design can withstand the spontaneity and creative force of the plan of God. Nature itself recognizes a man in flight from God and attempts to return the man to God.

The storm leaves the sailors aghast. These veterans of the shipping lanes had seen many a storm, but this one is different. Like the prophet it tracks, this storm spans both eternity and time. It does not follow a predictable path. The sailors haven't seen a storm like this before, so fear overcomes them "and each cried to his god" (Jon 1:5). "They threw the cargo that was in the ship into the sea, to lighten it for them" (Jon 1:5). The storm is not only after Job; it is drawing others in its wake. Their first instinct in such deathly fear is to pray. Yet they pray to false gods. Then they turn to the cargo, to all those things that only a day before they found valuable. They turn to the goods of the marketplace, the merchandise and the trinkets, all those things for which the world is willing to pay a price. And, just as God "hurled a great wind upon the sea," they now hurl the cargo into the same depths. They do not realize what they are doing. They hope only to lighten the load, to allow the ship, once unencumbered of excess weight, to float higher above the mountainous waves. It seems as if they steal from one false god, the god of commerce, to appease another false god, Neptune.

But something deeper is happening. They are throwing the false goods of the world into the wind that is sweeping upon the surface of the deep, which is to say, *into the very creative action of God*. They are, on a level they are not even yet dimly aware, throwing their old way of life away. The storm has revealed something to them. The old will not last, and simply will not do. They cannot simply turn away from it. They must cast it off completely. God is teaching them. "You cannot serve both God and mammon."

And, true to form, the prophet is different. He is not on the same track as everyone else. When the world panics, the prophet sleeps: "Jonah, meanwhile, had gone down into the hold of the ship and had lain down, and was fast asleep" (Jon 1:5). The same storm that drives the world into disorder lulls the prophet to sleep. And the sleep is not a mere nap. Prophets *know*. Jonah *knew* the storm was coming not from the change in atmospheric pressure, the blustery winds, or the grim gathering clouds. He knew it because he knew God, and the word of God had come to him. When we run from God, he sends a storm. As Jonah felt the wind and saw the billowing clouds, he tightened his collar and thought, "Right on schedule." He went down into the ship's hull and ran into his last hiding place: sleep.

Again, like the creation account, the sleep of Jonah is similar to that of Adam (see Gn 2:21). In the Bible, sleep is no ordinary experience. It always precedes the great creative action of God. Abram falls into a trance prior to the conversation with God (see Gn 15:12). Young Samuel awakens from his sleep and cries out, "Speak, for your servant is listening" (1 Sam 3:10). Job knew this same truth: "Amid thoughts from visions of the night, when deep sleep falls on mortals" (Job 4:13), and again, "In a dream, in a vision of the night . . . then he opens their ears" (Job 33:15–16). The apostles fall asleep in the Garden of Gethsemane during the agony of Jesus (see Lk 22:45). Sleep is the sign that Jonah has finally died to his former self and awaits the awaking touch of God.

The captain wakes Jonah with the ironic question: "What are you doing sound asleep?" (Jon 1:6). Something is going on in Jonah. The irony deepens, like the water all around them. The captain pleads with Jonah to call on his god, as the sailors are doing, so that "Perhaps the god will spare us a thought so that we do not perish" (Jon 1:6). This was Jonah's original task. When he runs from God, he turns around into God. This is the story of the Christian life.

Next, as the soldiers at the crucifixion will do, the sailors turn to lots to decide their next move: "Come, let us cast lots, so that we may know on whose account this calamity has come upon us" (Jon 1:7). When throwing the cargo overboard fails, when calling on their false gods fails, the sailors turn to chance. Jonah, whose luck simply does not hold, cannot hide even in pure chance. The lot falls to Jonah (cf. Jon 1:7). Everything points to the prophet, and he confesses: "I worship the LORD, the God of heaven, who made the sea and the dry land" (Jon 1:9). The storm, the waves, and the dark sky are scary enough, but now this weathered and seasoned crew is "even more afraid . . . the men knew that he was fleeing from the presence of the LORD" (Jon 1:10). And in their fear, they turn again to the prophet, "What shall we do to you, that the sea may quiet down for us?" (Jon 1:11). They want desperately Jonah to prophesize now for them.

The prophet is clear: "Pick me up and throw me into the sea; then the sea will quiet down for you; for I know it is because of me that this great storm has come upon you" (Jon 1:12). Jonah evangelizes the crew. They pray to the true God, "Please, O LORD, we pray, do not let us perish on account of this man's life . . . for you, LORD, have done as it pleased you" (Jon 1:14). Not only do they pray, but they now have knowledge of God's designs and plans. Still later they will make vows (see Jon 1:16). But first, they hurl Jonah into the sea (see Jon 1:15). The sea finally grows calm. The storm disappears, going back where it came from—*inside Jonah*. It is as if the prophet prophesizes to the sea, and the ocean itself is converted. The prophet was, as always, the missing ingredient. What he has done for the sea, he must now do for Nineveh. Yet he has to take one more step.

"But the LORD provided a large fish to swallow up Jonah; and Jonah was in the belly of the fish three days and three nights" (Jon 1:17). Cast into the sea, Jonah goes deeper still. What is this mysterious great fish? The early Christians identified themselves with Christ. Symbolically, the way they did this was to use his name and his two great titles: "Jesus Christ Son of God Savior." The Greek spelling for this phrase is Ιησους Χριστος Θεου Υιος Σωτηρ (*Iēsous Christos Theou Huios Sōter*). The early Christians would take the first letter of each word: ΙΧΘΥΣ (*ichthus*), pronounced ikthus. The first letters of the name and titles of Jesus spell out the Greek word for fish, so the fish became a symbol for the Christian. The theological writer Tertullian explains that the Christian was born in the waters of baptism and is therefore safe only in abiding in the water permanently.[11] The water is the saving action of Christ found in the life of grace begun in Baptism. This meant abiding in Christ, because *Christ is the fish*. He alone is the one who floods the arid and desert places of sin with his abundant life of supernatural grace. Jonah has nowhere left to run. He is literally thrown into a type of the waters of Baptism, where he meets God. Just as Jesus was in the tomb three days, so Jonah is configured to Christ by his ordeal.

It may be hard for us to swallow, but if you and I are running from doubts, questions, struggles, and fears, if we find ourselves in exile or turmoil, if the old ways aren't working anymore and the new pressures are intense, if the storm is

---

11. Tertullian, *De Baptismo*.

rising, then we may actually be poised on the brink of deep transformation. Our trials and journeys, once united to Christ, become the setting for our journey to holiness and sanctification.

CHAPTER SEVEN

The Great Catch of Fish

Once while Jesus was standing beside the lake of Gennesaret, and the crowd was pressing in on him to hear the word of God, he saw two boats there at the shore of the lake; the fishermen had gone out of them and were washing their nets. He got into one of the boats, the one belonging to Simon, and asked him to put out a little way from the shore. Then he sat down and taught the crowds from the boat. When he had finished speaking, he said to Simon, "Put out into the deep water and let down your nets for a catch." Simon answered, "Master, we have worked all night long but have caught nothing. Yet if you say so, I will let down the nets." When they had done this, they caught so many fish that their nets were beginning to break. So they signaled their partners in the other boat to come and help them. And they came and filled both boats, so that they began to sink. But when Simon Peter saw it, he fell down at Jesus' knees, saying, "Go away from me, Lord, for I am a sinful man!" For he and all who were with him were amazed at the catch of fish that they had taken; and so also were James and John, sons of Zebedee, who were partners with Simon. Then Jesus said to Simon, "Do not be afraid; from now on you will be catching people." When they had brought their boats to shore, they left everything and followed him. (Lk 5:1–11)

How many times Simon squinted at the horizon. How many times his well-tanned face gazed at the seas as he wondered: "Where is the great catch, that secret fishing hole, that will fill my nets, fill my family's stomachs, fill my pockets, and fill my career?" How many times Simon had squinted at those waves, waiting and watching! And he wished for nothing more than to find that spot, so that he could finally relax and consider himself worthwhile.

And then this day dawned. The crowd "was pressing in on him" (Lk 5:1). The Greek word for "pressed in on" used here is *epikeisthai*. Saint Luke will later use this same word to describe the crowd as they press forward on Good Friday calling for the crucifixion of Jesus (see Lk 23:23). But today the crowd presses in, "to hear the word of God" (Lk 5:1).

At the same time, the fishermen "were washing their nets." Later, Jesus will wash their feet and cleanse them from their sin (see Jn 13:4–11), and also, as Saint Paul will say, by the washing of the Word (see Eph 5:26).

Then Jesus steps into Simon's boat and sits down, taking the traditional posture of the teacher. The significance is twofold. First, Simon Peter's boat symbolizes the Church: the Lord has given to Peter the keys of the kingdom and the power to bind and to loose (see Mt 16:13–20; cf. Jn 21:15–19). Second, it is from the Church, the boat of Peter, that the Lord teaches. When Jesus asks Simon to push out into the water, he responds, "Lord, we worked hard all night. We tried to do it our way. I've been lowering these nets all my life. I know every inch of this lake. If there are fish out there, I can find them." Then he says: "Yet if you say so, I will let down the nets" (Lk 5:5). Simon Peter lowers the nets *at the word* of Jesus. The Greek expression used for "word" here is *rhēmati*, which means *at the utterance of your living voice*. Notice the docility of Peter. The crowd "was pressing in . . . to hear the word of God" (Lk 5:1), but it is Peter who is ready to obey this living word.

Up to this point Simon had worked "all night," which is to say, he had worked in sin and darkness. And sin and darkness worked for him, for a while. He had enough money to buy the best, most sturdy net. As he spread his hands across that net he thought, "One day this will be full, in fact, one day it will overflow." And that net worked for a while, until he had enough money to go and spread his hands across the bow of the boat and thought, "This is the one that will take me deeper into the sea, farther from shore, and closer to the spot with all the fish." And he put the net and the boat together. He succeeded; he made ends meet. But before meeting Jesus, he was still working in the darkness. Something about his net and his boat, indeed his very life, was not yet converted. But then Jesus stepped into the boat and into his life and said, "Put out into the deep water and let down your nets for a catch" (Lk 5:4). Ordinarily Simon would say, "You're foolish. I'm the expert. No one does it that way."

But something in Simon is changing.

Something in Simon *knows* that if this Jesus says to do something that sounds foolish, that the crew would laugh at, that Simon knows will never work because he's tried it, then he says, "Yes, at your command, I'll do it."

And so he went out and he lowered the nets. Then he saw something in the nets. He began to think, "The net is full . . . this looks like a good catch. Is this a fluke?" He looks closely. "The nets are filling up quickly . . . I have never seen them *this full*." He grins widely and begins to laugh and even shout: "I have it made . . . I've found the spot . . . I'm set . . . this is the haul." He orders the crew to haul in the nets. But . . . *wait a moment.* Simon thinks, "Wait. What's happening? The nets are *ripping* . . . they're *tearing* . . . Those nets can't *break* . . . they're my livelihood!" In fact the original Greek word indicates that the nets actually broke, in the sense of being rent asunder. It is as if the bursting of the nets represents a decisive break with Simon's old way of life.

Then Simon pulls the nets into the boat, that boat *into* which he had put all his sweat, blood, and tears, the boat he had worked for, saved for, and slaved over. The *boat* started to get so full that Simon had to send for another boat and more fishermen. After he suddenly hit the jackpot, the boat started to *sink.* First, the net was bursting, and now the boat was bursting. Nothing can contain the power of Jesus. Everything Simon depended on to keep him afloat started to sink. They *had* to get to shore. Later he would remember how odd it all was. Everything he had ever wanted started to fill that boat. All the fish pouring in . . . and now Simon could see that success, as the world defines it, was the *worst thing* that had ever happened to him. He had gotten his own way, but now the nets were breaking as the boat struggled to stay afloat.

Simon had nowhere else to turn, so he turned to Jesus. Simon had fallen to his knees before a lot of things in his life: his career, his reputation, his vanity, and most of all, that net and that boat. And now he fell at the knees of the one Person who could finally make sense of Simon's life. Many others had fallen at the knees of Jesus: the unclean spirits (see Mk 3:11; Lk 8:28), and the people who seek healing (see Mk 5:33; 7:25; Lk 8:47). Although he was already prepared to obey Jesus (see Lk 5:5), Simon is now simply overwhelmed. Jesus has taken him farther than any boat ever could. Simon, the fisherman who used to gaze at the horizon, has now crossed the horizon *within himself* . . . and to the Lord. And Simon said, "Go away from me, Lord, for I am a sinful man!" (Lk 5:8). Jesus forgives him. And it dawns on Simon, "This is the One who *created* those fish. It wasn't my ingenuity and skill. It wasn't my net or my boat. This is the One. And he can do it all day long. But Jesus is not interested in doing that, so why am I?" And Jesus, in this dawning moment, calls Simon to follow him (see Lk 5:10). Then the great miracle happens: Simon stands before the nets and the boat, and he abandons them. He walks away. Why? He fell in love.

We can be a lot like Simon. We are professionals. We work in Manhattan, Washington, D.C., Chicago, or out on the coast. We wear the uniforms, the styles, the brand names of our "with-it" culture. We have lots of "nets and boats" that we certainly aren't done paying for. We play the part. We want to get "there" quickly while we leave others behind. We take these attitudes from our work and begin to live our marriages this way. We treat our spouse like a thing and our family like a business. Society has taken some very good people and driven them on a very different course. Our contemporary mentality is ready to destroy life and love.

But then we see something. We see the gift. We start to see the light of Jesus Christ. The looks on our faces begin to change. We look like people beginning to awake from a nightmare. And we think, "Why didn't anyone tell us this before?" We have gone to church and perhaps even had a religious education. Why didn't anyone tell us that the only answer to life is a total gift of self? Anything else will overload our nets to the point of anxiety, chaos, and pain. We give this to other people, and then the nets break and the boat sinks. We need to leave our nets and our boats. We need to go out. Only Jesus Christ can heal the wounds of society and our personal sin. Given the hard-heartedness of so many, it may take a generation to heal the effects of society's ills over the last forty years. That generation is *this* generation. The great catch may look wonderful on paper, but when it sits in our living room, it will tear us down.

But we can see another horizon: the Culture of Life and the Civilization of Love that see the person, who is called to make a total gift of self. All it takes is falling at the knees of Jesus. He alone, in and through his Church, gives us the strength that allows us to let go of the nets, take up the cross, and follow him.

CHAPTER EIGHT

The Cleansing of a Leper

In the morning, while it was still very dark, he got up and went out to a deserted place, and there he prayed. And Simon and his companions hunted for him. When they found him, they said to him, "Everyone is searching for you." He answered, "Let us go on to the neighboring towns, so that I may proclaim the message there also; for that is what I came out to do." And he went throughout Galilee, proclaiming the message in their synagogues and casting out demons.

A leper came to him begging him, and kneeling he said to him, "If you choose, you can make me clean." Moved with pity, Jesus stretched out his hand and touched him, and said to him, "I do choose. Be made clean!" Immediately the leprosy left him, and he was made clean. After sternly warning him he sent him away at once, saying to him, "See that you say nothing to anyone; but go, show yourself to the priest, and offer for your cleansing what Moses commanded, as a testimony to them." But he went out and began to proclaim it freely, and to spread the word, so that Jesus could no longer go into a town openly, but stayed out in the country; and people came to him from every quarter. (Mk 1:35–45)

Jesus decided it was time to leave. He was, by all accounts, an early riser. So early in his public ministry, when his work was finished in Capernaum, the Gospel of Mark tells us, "In the morning, while it was still very dark, he got up and went out to a deserted place, and there he prayed" (Mk 1:35). The word that the Gospel uses for "very early" is *lian*. This word does not simply mean earlier than usual. It means "exceedingly early" or "exceedingly beyond measure." The same word is used to describe the color of the garments of Jesus at the transfiguration: "and his clothes became dazzling white, such as no one on earth could bleach them" (Mk 9:3). In the transfiguration the garments of our Lord were white beyond measure. So too, something about his rising and going off to pray is beyond measure. The Greek word used here for "rising," *anastas*, is the same that will be used when Jesus teaches that he would rise on the third day (see Mk 9:9; 9:31). Finally, it is the same used to describe the resurrection see Mk 16:9). Already on this Capernaum morning, early in his public ministry, in even the seemingly mundane actions of Jesus, we find a foreshadowing of his victory on Easter morning.

And so, Jesus leaves one town to go to another. As he nears the outskirts of the town, someone approaches: "A leper came to him begging him, and kneeling he said to him, 'If you choose, you can make me clean'" (Mk 1:40). Lepers were not allowed to live in the town because their disease was highly contagious and disfiguring. According to the Book of Leviticus, the leprous person, with sores, blotches, scabs, and pustules, was unclean, and as such had to dwell apart and live outside the city or camp (see Lv 13:1–2; 44–46). As an outcast, the leper must wander on the outskirts. Persons with leprosy lost not only their health but also everything else: family, friends, work. These were all replaced with fear, especially the fear that others had of being infected. The people of the town, however, did not abandon the leper outright: the only thing worse than having lepers in their town was having lepers on their consciences. And the crowd always has a rather slim conscience. The leper lives *outside* the town, close enough to beg for scraps. Close enough so that people won't feel guilty, but far enough to avoid any risk so that everyone will be safe. As the psalmist said, "Some wandered in desert wastes, finding no way to an inhabited town.... Then they cried to the LORD in their trouble, and he delivered them from their distress" (Ps 107:4, 6). Everyone knew that lepers also were not permitted to approach people, because anyone they touched became physically and spiritually unclean. The psalmist says in his distress and loneliness, "My friends and companions stand aloof from my affliction" (Ps 38:12). Recall the account of the ten lepers who met Jesus: "As he [Jesus] entered a village, ten lepers approached him. Keeping their distance, they called out, saying, "Jesus, Master, have mercy on us!'" (Lk 17:12–13). They raise their voice to cover the distance institutionalized between them and Jesus. No leper would have been permitted near the crowd when "the whole town was gathered at the door."

The sinful human tendency to divide and label, to cast out and to reject, is a sickness deeper than disease. The rule is simple: the leper cannot join the crowd. But the word, like leprosy, can spread. Word of many healings Jesus performed has even reached the isolated leper colony on the margin of society.

On the outskirts of our mind, do we believe we are on the margins? Does the phrase wander somewhere within us: "*If only* Jesus would take away the anxiety, the depression, the disease, the loss and pain? If I met him, he would heal me? But healing seems impossible." And we wander. So too, did the lepers.

Once Jesus decided it was time to leave that town, in more ways than one he stepped into the "in-between" place. Geographically he is passing from one town to another, crossing the barren land. The terrible and dangerous place of no-man's-land is the shameful distance that can exist even in a person's heart: the last place anything new would ever emerge. Jesus passes from one society to another, from one level of sickness to another. His journey, like his mission, is taking him deeper into humanity's ills and divisions, to those on the margins. Yesterday he healed the physical ailments of the townspeople. Today he will heal their spiritual ailments. He steps onto the edge, taking them where they would rather not follow. Jesus meets the leper. Or rather, the leper meets him on the edge in the well-hidden place of shame.

And the first thing the leper does is break the rule. The leper "came to him" (Mk 1:40). But the leper has heard the news: "This Jesus heals. Yesterday he healed *everyone.*" The leper had no future. He was contaminated. His disease would continue to spread throughout his body. And the worse it got, the more people would avoid him and reject him. He had no way out. "Could Jesus heal me? I've tried doctor after doctor, remedy after remedy . . . Why make a fool of myself again?" The leper began to believe the news, then he began to hope. And hope breaks all the rules. The leper overcame his hesitation and reservation as he saw Jesus approach from a distance: the old imposed, required, deadly distance. Don't take one more step—or else. Then the leper did something he was told and trained not to do: He dared. He had almost forgotten how to take a risk. He saw something about Jesus, even in the awful distance. The rumors and stories, the word from yesterday all began to fit when he saw Jesus . . . *especially* across the distance. He did not just *see* the healer, but he *gazed on the Savior.* And the leper could not contain himself. He "came to him" (Mk 1:40). His deeper healing, and that of the town, is beginning as Jesus enters into the place of shame.

We encounter the place of shame too, a place we go more often than we admit. We happen upon the place of shame every day. We pretend we look good on the outside, but we have something inside that we attempt to hide from other people. We cover it with cosmetics, our portfolio, our attitudes, and ways of speaking. We may hide it and pretend it isn't there, but it still generates a lot of energy. What is the place of shame in our life? When others attempt to shame us they always try to make it sound polite, almost like assistance. Yet, we feel the shame start to spread in the pit of our stomach when a friend says to us, "Well, that meal was great, except next time you should add . . ." or our in-laws say, "You live in a nice neighborhood, but the only problem is . . ." or a friend says, "You're getting into a great line of work, but do you really think you'll be able to . . ." Others attempt to control us through shame. They trick us into trying to respond to their shame, and we put on a fake personality to come out of the shame. When we try to please others, we adapt to artificial ways that are not our own but have become so familiar that they seem to be real. When we hear the word "except" or "but," the moment of shame arrives. Imagine if the next time someone attempted to shame us, you or I spoke up and said, "Excuse me, but I'm not going to let you shame me today." Imagine *if we actually said that.* If we did, the weight would be lifted, and we would feel an infusion of strength. The curse would be lifted and a blessing would descend. Where shame was before, Jesus now declares healing, just as he did for the leper.

The leper kneels before Jesus (see Mk 1:40). Even in his illness and desperation, the leper *realizes something* about the Person of Jesus. "If you choose, you can make me clean" (Mk 1:40). The leper recognizes that the healing power of Jesus lies in his will. Nothing else is required but that Jesus *deem* it to be so. In various Gospel passages we learn that Jesus did touch some of those whom he healed. Others he healed simply by his word, without any indication of touch. Here the leper seems to say "if you simply will it, you can heal me." And indeed, Jesus can. But the Gospel tells us, "Moved with pity, Jesus *stretched out his hand,* and *touched him*, and said to him, 'I do choose. Be made clean!'" (Mk 1:41; emphasis added). Now Jesus is the one breaking the rules. Jesus dared push against the limits of the deadly status quo. Their eyes locked. Jesus *touched* the *leper*. That was forbidden; against the rules. Like the leper, Jesus has crossed the forbidden distance. The leper "came to him" and now, as he will do on the cross, Jesus "stretched out his hand" (Mk 1:41). The leper broke the rules. Jesus broke the rules, too, by touching him. Why didn't Jesus simply heal this leper without a touch, as he healed other lepers (cf. Lk 17:13–15)? Because the disease was so contagious, once someone touched a leper that person became unclean. Jesus could have cured the leper just by willing it, without a touch. Even the leper knew as much. So did Jesus, for he said, "I do choose. Be made clean!" (Mk 1:41): The providential antidote flows forth at the word and touch of Jesus. And the leper is cured: "Immediately the leprosy left him, and he was made clean" (Mk 1:42). The word of Jesus is *immediate*. The word of Jesus now *overtakes* all the other words the leper has heard *about* Jesus. Now, the leper receives the word of Jesus: "Be made clean" (Mk 1:41).

As Jesus stretched out his hand, he was "moved with pity" (Mk 1:41). The Greek word used in the text is *splanchnistheis*, a very significant word. It means not simply that Jesus felt sorry for the man, but that Jesus was moved in his innermost places with compassion. In fact, this movement, in the sense intended by this word, is a birth image.[1] Jesus, moved with compassion,

---

1. See Jean Laffitte, "Love and Forgiveness," Livio Melina and Carl Anderson, eds., in *The Way of Love: Reflections on Pope Benedict XVI's Encyclical "Deus Caritas Est"* (San Francisco: Ignatius Press, 2006), 177. See also Hans Urs von Balthasar, *The Glory of the Lord I*, 243, 389, and his *The Glory of the Lord VII*, 86; Erasmo Leiva-Merikakis, *Fire of Mercy, Heart of the Word: Meditations on the Gospel According to Saint Matthew*, vol. 1 (San Francisco: Ignatius Press, 1996), 197; Simon Tugwell, *The Beatitudes: Soundings in Christian Tradition* (London: Darton, Longman, and Todd, Ltd., 1985), 94; Oliver Davies, *A Theology of Compassion: Metaphysics of Difference and the Renewal of Tradition* (Grand Rapids, MI: Eerdmans Press, 2001), 247–248.

is pouring himself out in effusive love. In one sense, his compassion is both a *breaking open* and a *sending forth* of his innermost life in love, and all this foreshadows the piercing of his side (see Jn 19:34). Something is emerging from Jesus as he stretches out his hand to this leper, just as he will be moved with compassion as he stretches forth his hand on the cross.

Next, Jesus sternly warns the leper to "say nothing to anyone; but go, show yourself to the priest, and offer for your cleansing what Moses commanded, as a testimony to them" (Mk 1:44). This firm warning of Jesus hints at society's awareness of the contagion. But the leper goes and makes the whole matter known publicly, "proclaim[ing] it freely" (Mk 1:45). The leper, now cleansed, is apparently welcome in polite society. The former leper now spreads the very word he had heard about the healing power of Jesus.

In a sense, the leper becomes an evangelist, yet something more is going on. Jesus broke the rules, and that has consequences. Jesus touched the one with the highly contagious disease. So now Jesus must remain outside and out of bounds: the Gospel tells us that "Jesus could no longer go into a town openly, but stayed out in the country . . ." (Mk 1:45). It's as if a reverse contagion has occurred. Public consequences follow the violation of a cultural taboo. Now the leper can enter the town and Jesus cannot; it's as if Jesus has taken the leper's place. In touching the leper, Jesus, in a sense, *became* the leper. Jesus now must remain outside. Why did Jesus *touch* the leper? Something deeper is moving in the plan and design of God: the town's deeper healing cresting toward completion. Remember Simon's words: "Everyone is searching for you" (Mk 1:37). Jesus might wonder: "Are they? How far will they follow me? Will they continue to play it safe, or will they follow me to the edge and beyond? Will they follow me across their fears? Their hatreds? Their rules?"

Jesus remains in the desert places. He remains where the lepers dwell. He stays on the margins, at the edge, in the last place. Note the final line of this Gospel passage: "He stayed out in the country; and *people came to him from every quarter*" (Mk 1:45; emphasis added). Their healing is now complete, for it has been transformed into *discipleship*: they no longer avoid the outskirts. All the consequences of touching the leper no longer matter. The people no longer hide behind their seemingly safe limits and push others to the margins. Now, because of the action of Jesus, they rush to the margins. It will never be easy, but, like Jesus, the people of that town decided it was time to leave. It was time to leave the old hatreds, fears, and labels. It was time to follow Jesus. And when they did, the deserted place thrived with new and abundant life.

CHAPTER NINE

The Wedding Feast of Cana

On the third day there was a wedding in Cana of Galilee, and the mother of Jesus was there. Jesus and his disciples had also been invited to the wedding. When the wine gave out, the mother of Jesus said to him, "They have no wine." And Jesus said to her, "Woman, what concern is that to you and to me? My hour has not yet come." His mother said to the servants, "Do whatever he tells you." Now standing there were six stone water jars for the Jewish rites of purification, each holding twenty or thirty gallons. Jesus said to them, "Fill the jars with water." And they filled them up to the brim. He said to them, "Now draw some out, and take it to the chief steward." So they took it. When the steward tasted the water that had become wine, and did not know where it came from (though the servants who had drawn the water knew), the steward called the bridegroom and said to him, "Everyone serves the good wine first, and then the inferior wine after the guests have become drunk. But you have kept the good wine until now." Jesus did this, the first of his signs, in Cana of Galilee, and revealed his glory; and his disciples believed in him. (Jn 2:1–11)

The preparations had been underway for a very long time, and now the day had arrived. The Gospel tells us the wedding was to take place "on the third day . . ." (Jn 2:1). The third day from when? Saint Bonaventure says it was the third day since the call of the disciples;[1] Saint Caesarius explains that the third day is a reference to the mystery of the Trinity.[2] The "third day" is also a reference to the resurrection of the Lord, which is his victory over sin and death. Already, at the beginning of Jesus's public ministry, there is a foreshadowing to the culmination of his mission in the cross and resurrection. Just like the wedding feast of Cana, the cross too is a type of wedding—it is the self-gift of Christ the Bridegroom to his Bride, the Church.[3] This idea is deepened when we look at the Greek word for "invited" used in the passage. The word is *eklēthē* and means "called." Jesus has been invited, or "called" to attend the wedding. Likewise, he is called by the Father from all eternity to offer himself in a gift of sacrificial love in his salvific mission. And so, at the very beginning of his public life, we already catch a glimpse of its zenith: on the third day, "there was a wedding in Cana of Galilee" (Jn 2:1).

The first verse introduces another similarity between Cana and the passion of the Lord. The Gospel notes that his mother is present at this wedding feast (see Jn 2:1). She will also be with him, standing beneath his cross (see Jn 19:25). Saint John stood at the foot of the Lord's cross as well, but the Gospel does not tell us if Saint John was at the wedding. The Church places

---

1. Saint Bonaventure, *Commentary on the Gospel of John* (Saint Bonaventure, NY: Franciscan Institute Publications, 2007), 140.

2. See Caesarius of Arles, *Sermons vol. II (81–186)* in *Fathers of the Church: A New Translation* (Washington DC: The Catholic University of America Press, 1947), vol. 47, 402–3.

3. Pope Benedict XVI notes this in *Jesus of Nazareth Part Two, Holy Week*, Kindle Edition, Chapter 6.2, Loc. 2848 of 4202.

great emphasis on the sermons of the Fathers of the Church and the saints, who specialize in a spiritual interpretation of the Sacred Scriptures. Saint Jerome and Saint Augustine, two Fathers of the Church, and Saint Bonaventure, a medieval scholastic theologian, taught that Saint John was indeed present at the wedding feast. In fact, they taught that he was the bridegroom, that the wedding was that of Saint John the Evangelist, and that the Lord and his mother are invited because they were related to Saint John.[4] At first we may be surprised to hear this because we frequently associate Saint John with the life of virginity. Saint Bonaventure points out that there is no contradiction between Saint John's being a virgin and also being married, as the marriage was a virginal marriage.[5]

A third parallel with the passion is introduced by the Lord himself. Cana is one of the rare places in the Gospels where we have the privilege of listening in on a conversation between the Lord and his Blessed Mother: "When the wine ran short, the mother of Jesus said to him, 'They have no wine.'" Our Lady intercedes, as always. The Lord responds that his "hour has not yet come" (Jn 2:4). Later, we will listen to another conversation between the Lord and his Blessed Mother, when the hour has arrived, as he hangs upon the cross: "When Jesus saw his mother and the disciple whom he loved standing beside her, he said to his mother, 'Woman, here is your son.' Then he said to the disciple, 'Here is your mother.' And from that hour the disciple took her into his own home" (Jn 19:26–27). Jesus refers to his mother as "woman" (*gynē*), both at the wedding feast of Cana (see Jn 2:4) and from the cross (see Jn 19:26). The *Catechism of the Catholic Church* notes that at Cana, Mary intercedes with

---

4. Saint Bonaventure, *Commentary on the Gospel of John*, 151.

5. Ibid., 152; on the historical custom and acceptance of a virgin and celibate man living together in marriage, see Jean Daniélou, *The Infancy Narratives*, 22.

her Son for the needs of the wedding feast, yet Cana is only the sign of the wedding of the Lamb, in which he offers his body and blood for his Bride the Church: It is at the hour of the New Covenant, at the foot of the cross (see Jn 19:25–27), that Mary is heard as the Woman, the new Eve, the true "Mother of all the living."[6] Cana and Calvary are much closer than we realize.

The cross can show up in the unlikeliest of moments. A marriage feast is supposed to be filled with joy and celebration. Yet, at Cana a crisis was developing rapidly. The waiters were down to their last case of wine—the *last* case. The maître d's heart began to pound. If the wine fails so will his reputation. The people will never stop talking about the day the wine ran dry. Banquets were his bread and butter. His reputation depended on them, and his business depended on his reputation. In a matter of moments all eyes would turn, disappointed, to him. At what was to be the height of the celebration, the crowd would be stranded. *There was no more wine.* The head waiter is playing a role in a much larger drama. The wine stands as a symbol for the fullness of life and the promise by which God vowed to deliver his people. His concern is the symbol of all the hopes of the human race that God would fulfill his pledge.

There appeared to be no solution. Certainly he had no time to fix the problem of having no more wine. The emptiness was inching ever closer. He wanted to shrink away, to be invisible. Word was spreading like a fuse to a powder keg: "They're out. All gone . . . they have no more wine." In which case, soon, they would have no more guests. The celebration and joy would be over. The wait staff all gathered around him as if to transfer any residual, misplaced responsibility to him. They knew that they, the first line of defense, would be the first to be blamed. They

---

6. *CCC*, no. 2618.

wanted to be close enough to point to him, to hand off the blame. Blame is the first sign that you do not have a plan.

And then he felt a tug at his sleeve. Oh . . . not *now*. Can't you see I am busy? He had been fielding requests *all day*. But a request in the midst of a crisis was an annoyance he could not abide. What do you *want*? Whatever concern you may have, it can't matter as much as *my* problem. We are out of *wine*. The very juice of the celebration is *gone* . . . vanished. He did not know where to turn.

It is a woman at his arm. Now as she tugs at his sleeve, she leans close and speaks, her voice calms with its very tone. At its sound his fever-pitch, mind-racing cares seem miles distant now. She has cast them away with a word. He has never heard a voice like this one. She blames no one. She knows of a plan. The plan is already underway, even in the midst of his confusion. In fact, the plan has been underway for millennia, since and before the beginning of time. The Son of God has come *to* a wedding, but has also come *for* a wedding. He, the Lord, *is* the Bridegroom at whose hour the wine of redemption for the human race will flow from his very side.[7] Now, as she nods in the direction of her Son, she speaks into the maître d's ear, beyond his crisis, to his deepest need: "*Do whatever he tells you*" (Jn 2:5).

Mary summons the miracle. It is her petition. Our Lady's petition becomes the instruction of the Lord to the servants to fill the ceremonial jars with water (see Jn 2:7). The servants obey, even though if one is desperately searching for wine to satisfy a large crowd, filling jars with water is not a high priority. Despite every inclination otherwise, despite their better judgment, despite the risk of appearing foolish, the servants are *filled with obedience*. Their panic became obedience at the word of

---

7. See Hans Urs von Balthasar, *Theo-Drama: Theological Dramatic Theory IV: The Action* (San Francisco: Ignatius Press, 1994), 235–236.

Mary. The Mother of the Lord has told them to "Do whatever he tells you" (Jn 2:5) because that is exactly what she has always done. And so their obedience continues. The Lord and his mother chose that only the *servants* would know the *source* of the miracle: only the servants knew where the water made wine came from (see Jn 2:9). And so, they, in turn, fill the jars. As the jars are filled, the water *itself* is filled. He who created water out of nothing now creates wine out of water. Later, at the Last Supper he will again preside over a transformation: not water into wine but wine into his blood.

So now the Lord commands that the first drought of the water-made-wine be served to the waiter-in-charge (see Jn 2:8). The servants again obey. When the waiter tastes the wine (see Jn 2:9), he calls the Bridegroom, who, in one sense, is Christ himself. The Greek word for "calls" (*phōnei*) is a different one from the word used earlier for the invitation to the wedding. This word, which brings us back to the passion, refers to the cock crowing. It is used when the Lord predicts the denial of Simon Peter, for the denial itself, and as Peter weeps afterward (see Mt 26:34; 26:74–75). The cock crowing symbolizes the time of the deeper abandonment of the Lord. It is when the cock crows that Christ, the Bridegroom is called and responds, and drinks the cup to the very depths and thus pours forth the wine of the New Covenant, as on the cross he offers himself for his Bride, the Church.[8]

---

8. See Saint Augustine, *Tractates on the Gospel of John 1–10* in *Fathers of the Church: A New Translation* (Washington, DC: The Catholic University of America Press, 1947), vol. 78, 182–83.

CHAPTER TEN

The Pharisee and the Tax Collector

He also told this parable to some who trusted in themselves that they were righteous and regarded others with contempt: "Two men went up to the temple to pray, one a Pharisee and the other a tax collector. The Pharisee, standing by himself, was praying thus, 'God, I thank you that I am not like other people: thieves, rogues, adulterers, or even like this tax collector. I fast twice a week; I give a tenth of all my income.' But the tax collector, standing far off, would not even look up to heaven, but was beating his breast and saying, 'God, be merciful to me, a sinner!' I tell you, this man went down to his home justified rather than the other; for all who exalt themselves will be humbled, but all who humble themselves will be exalted." (Lk 18:9–14)

Two men went to the temple to pray—but the similarities end there. One of them was a tax collector, who stayed in the back and said little as he prayed. The other man was a Pharisee. He went immediately to the front and "took up his position." He knew all the prayers by heart. He knew all the laws and all the traditions, and had seemingly followed them all perfectly. All, that is, but one.

The Gospel subtly describes the Pharisee's prayer, telling us not that he prayed the psalms or other prayers, but that he prayed *to himself*. It does not mean he said the prayer *quietly*, whispered or mumbled the words in a low voice. No, the Gospel tells us that *he prayed to himself*. And notice the first word of his prayer: "God." The Pharisee prays *to himself* and begins with the name *God*. Simply put, the Pharisee thought he was God. That is his first sin. He breaks the first commandment: "Have no strange Gods before me." The Pharisee thinks himself God, and he rules from his throne there in the temple and wherever else he happens to be. And he looks over everyone else and makes decisions. Yet, his prayer, misdirected to himself, becomes even stranger.

The Pharisee prays, "God, I thank you that I am not like other people" (Lk 18:11). When most people pray, they do the opposite: they *wish they were* like everyone else. Some even begin to worry if they are not like everyone else. This gives us an insight into the Pharisee. The Gospel tells us that Jesus addressed this parable "to some who trusted in themselves that they were righteous and regarded others with contempt" (Lk 18:9). Going beyond simply not liking others or even hating them, the Pharisee regards others *with contempt*. Contempt is a pervasive scornful attitude that views others as if they were inferior. Contempt rolls its eyes with disdain and shakes its head with derision at what others have to say. Contempt thinks that it is superior to everyone else. And so the Pharisee prays: "I thank you that I am not like other people" (Lk 18:11). His "prayer" is a narcissistic meditation absorbed in who *he* is rather than who God is. In this, the Pharisee shows contempt not just for men but for God.

The Pharisee continues to describe for God the ways in which he differs from everyone else: he is not like "thieves, rogues, adulterers . . ." (Lk 18:11). Apparently, he has been look-ing around quite a bit and taking stock. For this Pharisee who prays to himself, everyone else is a sinner. He believes that he alone is superior to everyone else. He gives thanks that he is not like the rest of men, and then he adds, "or even like this tax col-lector" (Lk 18:11). Evidently, the Pharisee did a lot more looking around as he marched forward. His head spins like a beam from a lighthouse sweeping the sea, always on the lookout. *How else would he be aware of the tax collector seated in the back?* Pride and contempt always *watch.* They look around to see, to measure, to compare. The Pharisee's tendency to control is never far from him, not even from his prayer. Instead of a surrender, his prayer is an attempt to control God.

Oddly enough, the Pharisee's prayer continues, almost as if he is going to confession *in reverse.* The Pharisee first tells God that he has *not* committed adultery, or lied, or stolen. In fact, the Pharisee tells God the sins *of others.* Then, the Pharisee arro-gantly presumes to give himself his own *penance,* which he has already completed: he pays tithes and he fasts (see Lk 18:12). The Pharisee has an odd way of praying.

Pride is the sin of the Pharisee. Long before we commit other sins such as gluttony, lust, greed, envy, anger, and sloth, we sense the temptation. We sense the early urge of the appetites attached to gluttony and lust. We sense the telltale craving of greed and the disdain of envy. We can sense anger boiling up, and sloth dragging us down. But pride is different. Saint Bernard of Clairvaux observes that the sin of pride can attack even those who seem to have conquered other sins.[1] Pride usually comes to its full fury only after we commit it. More than any other sin,

---

1. Saint Bernard of Clairvaux, "Homily for the Fourth Sunday After Pentecost" in *Sermons for the Summer Season: Liturgical Sermons from Rogationtide to Pentecost* (Kalamazoo, MI: Cistercian Publications, 1990), 115–116.

pride *ambushes* us. With pride we sense an achievement we want to celebrate. We earned good grades, succeeded with a project, or planned an effective event. Yet as this good deed lingers in our memory, we want *more* from it, more than it was designed to give. We want it to fill up the intangible place in us that seems so empty for some reason. We want to get mileage out of it for our own self-esteem. We turn the event from a gift for others into fuel for ourselves. And we brag, show off, and drop hints: "Yes, that really went well . . . I didn't think that would work at all . . . It was much better than last year." Pride declares that the good work already achieved is somehow not enough. Pride makes us desire the pleasure of praise, and pushes us to congratulate ourselves rather than highlight the good that is done. The antidote for pride is honest thanksgiving that recognizes that all things belong to God. He alone is to be praised. Silence and quiet are the form of thanksgiving that reaches God's ears: "God opposes the proud, but gives grace to the humble" (Jas 4:6). Pride is especially deceptive and has very few early warning signs. Pride lurks behind our accomplishments and slips in at the last moment, pushing us to overestimate them. This last-minute ambush of pride was one of the reasons the early monks of the desert trained themselves for discernment, to note what began to arise in their thoughts.[2] Bede the Venerable urges us to act quickly the very moment the thought of sin arises in our heart.[3] If we allow it to linger, the thought that leads to sin will take firmer hold of our heart. The great spiritual writers of our tradition have long urged that the most effective way to cast off temptation is to pray the name of Our Lord or Our Lady.

---

2. See John Cassian, *The Conferences*, I. XX. 6 to I. XXII. 1 (61–63); and II.II.4–5 (84–85).

3. Bede the Venerable, *Homilies on the Gospels Book Two: Lent to the Dedication of the Church* (Kalamazoo, MI: Cistercian Publications, 1991), 116.

The temptation to pride often begins with the tug to compare or measure ourselves with and against others. Comparing, however, is quite different from competition, which can be healthy. Saint Paul even uses the image of competition to describe the Christian life (see 1 Cor 9:24–27; 2 Tm 4:7). But comparing—the tendency to measure ourselves and others—is rarely healthy and can lead us away from the call to holiness. We can almost unconsciously begin to size up and compare ourselves with other people on a daily basis. Comparing can become a lifestyle. It is as if we have to first gauge how popular or intelligent other people are, where their children attend school, what type of work they do, and the salary they make. Then we make sure we have the same, if not more. And then we call it "being myself." Yet, no matter how much we may seem to have, *as soon as we compare we lose.* We lose because *we found it necessary to compare in the first place.* Comparing is also the common cold of the spiritual life because no matter how much we compare, we always come up short. Even when comparing fails, we do not give up. Instead, after all the efforts we have made for success in the world fail, we turn to God and ask him to deliver on those things we feel we need so as to come out on top.

God, however, is love (see 1 Jn 4:8). Love does not give us everything we want, but love gives us everything we need. Sometimes God operates in ways we would otherwise not expect. His love is at work in what seems to us the most unlikely places. The tax collector, also known as a publican, didn't just collect taxes but extracted them. He was probably dishonest and greedy. People didn't like him. He had done his fair share of comparing as well. His life was a series of accounts. Greed often arises out of fear, so the tax collector was most likely full of fear, afraid to give anything away. Maybe old memories haunted him: his father might have told him, "You'll never get ahead . . . everything you touch breaks . . . you'll never amount to anything." Maybe the tax collector was so afraid he felt he had to be greedy simply to stay afloat and feed his family. Maybe he was unfair, corrupt, and adulterous, as the Pharisee judged.

But the tax collector has one thing that the Pharisee does not: the tax collector *knows how to go to God*. Even with his sin, pain, and bad habits, the tax collector remains *humble* and fears God.

The tax collector enters the temple, stays in the back, and does not even raise his eyes to heaven. He bows his head in the presence of God. In fact, if we were to ask him, the tax collector would most likely tell us that *he* does not know how to approach God. In his natural humility he probably thought that the Pharisee was the expert in prayer and had his life together.[4] When he went to pray, the tax collector did not look around like the Pharisee. He allowed nothing else to distract him from God's presence. Why did he bow his head and not raise his eyes to heaven? He did so because that was the typical prayer posture for a Jew of his time. One did not raise one's eyes to heaven because God is in heaven. Bowing one's head was the posture by which one observed the first commandment. The one who bows before the presence of the Lord knows very well that *he himself* is *not* God. Keeping one's head bowed also helps to maintain silence before the God who is so great.

The tax collector may have his sins and weakness, his faults and bad habits, but despite all that he has humility: he can finally come to the place where he knows and reveres the distance between himself and God. He beats his breast and asks, "God, be merciful to me, a sinner!" (Lk 18:13). Why does he beat his breast? He does so for at least two reasons: First, it demonstrates his sorrow for sin when he brings his sins before

---

4. See Vincent McNabb, OP, *The Craft of Prayer* (London: Burns, Oates and Washbourne, 1935), 77.

God. Second, he knows that his heart needs to wake up even more to the presence of God. The sins he has committed and his self-preoccupation can foster greed and lust, lulling the heart to sleep. He must awaken his heart. Even with his sins, in his humility the tax collector knows how to go before God.

We may sense a distance in our own life. We may feel as if all the plans we made when we were young have taken a tragic detour, that our old habits and frequent sins have disqualified and tainted us forever. Perhaps we stopped going to Mass a long time ago. Maybe we even stopped praying. We might be embarrassed to start to practice the faith again, though we have felt the urge several times. We may believe that the distance is too great and the journey too far, that God has given up on us, so we should do the same. But instead of being a sign of failure, the distance must be transformed into God's training ground. The urge we feel to practice the faith again does not come from us. It comes from God, from the Holy Spirit. God wants to meet us, to reach out to us, even in our own self-created distance, even across the painful distance of sin.

Only God can fill the distance between us and him, no matter what has led to the divide. God can forgive us and fill even the distance brought about by greed, dishonesty, and adultery. God can reach in and find us even when we have forgotten him, when we have neglected him, being caught up in the world's illusions, in the twists and turns of life. No matter what has forged the distance between us, and no matter how far it goes, God can fill it. This is why the tax collector opens the door and steps inside the temple. He is not ready to walk to the front. He might never feel ready for that. The tax collector *knows* that God can *fill* the distance with abundance. God fills it with mercy. For us, the confessional, the Reconciliation chapel, is often located in the back of church. God does not come to yell at us, to wag a finger at us, or say, "I told you so." He does not wait for us to make the first move, make a resolution, or get our life in order. He knows well how fragile we are. He comes to us even when we have turned from him. God crosses the distance, changing it so that it becomes a place for God to extend love even farther, to a new place: to us *in our distance* from him. And God delights to bridge that gap. The tax collector came and humbly took one small, faltering step into the distance between him and God. He bowed his head, beat his breast, and invited God's mercy into his heart, his soul, and his actions. He knew how to go to God.

CHAPTER ELEVEN

"Zaccheus, Come Down"

He entered Jericho and was passing through it. A man was there named Zaccheus; he was a chief tax collector and was rich. He was trying to see who Jesus was, but on account of the crowd he could not, because he was short in stature. So he ran ahead and climbed a sycamore tree to see him, because he was going to pass that way. When Jesus came to the place, he looked up and said to him, "Zaccheus, hurry and come down; for I must stay at your house today." So he hurried down and was happy to welcome him. All who saw it began to grumble and said, "He has gone to be the guest of one who is a sinner." Zaccheus stood there and said to the Lord, "Look, half of my possessions, Lord, I will give to the poor; and if I have defrauded anyone of anything, I will pay back four times as much." Then Jesus said to him, "Today salvation has come to this house, because he too is a son of Abraham. For the Son of Man came to seek out and to save the lost." (Lk 19:1–10)

Zacchaeus had never seen anything like this before. Far from being an average tax collector, he was a chief tax collector. Saint Cyril of Alexandria notes that this means Zacchaeus was completely consumed by greed.[1] This is the type of greed that Saint Paul refers to as idolatry (see Col 3:5). And then the Gospels adds redundantly: "He was a wealthy man." The people of that town knew Zacchaeus. He was the reason they couldn't afford to buy enough food or more sheep for the flock; he was the reason their parents argued about money. They knew what he looked like, and resented Zacchaeus for using the muscle of Rome against his own people. Yes, he could charge any percentage he wanted, but he was cheating his own people. That is why tax collectors were seen as no better than murderers and blasphemers. It wasn't simply greed—Zacchaeus passed ordinary greed years ago—but his lack of fidelity to his own people. His greed became idolatry; he worshiped Rome, and Rome paid well for his worship.

But as rich as he was, for as many doors as his money had opened, Zacchaeus had never seen anything like *this* before: "I have heard about this Jesus . . . he attracts crowds . . . thousands of people . . . he has influence . . . but . . . is it true he said that he has nowhere to lay his head? How can this man be so popular and not be rich? Why don't so many follow me? After all, I am rich . . . I have power and connections. Why do so many follow him? What connections does he have?" Zacchaeus was eager to see Jesus. Something had broken through all his defenses. Despite his wealth, reputation, and power, Zacchaeus found something attractive about the love of the Lord. Saint Bonaventure points out that the eagerness of Zacchaeus arises from prevenient grace, that grace that comes to us prior to any

---

1. See Saint Cyril of Alexandria, *Commentary on Luke, Homily 127*, trans., R. Payne Smith, (New York: Studion Publishers, 1983), 505.

effort or meritorious action of our own will, and draws us to the Lord and makes possible our response to his love.[2] Jesus tells us, "No one can come to me unless drawn by the Father who sent me" (Jn 6:44).

Others had felt this tug at their heart: the apostles and disciples whom Jesus called, Nicodemus the Pharisee who came to Jesus at night (see Jn 3:1–21). Even Pilate brushes close when he admits he finds no guilt in Jesus (see Jn 18:38), but we are not told if Pilate ever responded to the invitation. And the young man who had many possessions went away sad at the words of Jesus (see Mt 19:22). We do not know if he later returned to accept the invitation.

But Zacchaeus did. He followed the attraction he felt in his heart for Jesus. In fact, Zacchaeus rushed after the Lord, but he couldn't see Jesus because of the crowd.

The crowd always introduces an obstacle. Zacchaeus was used to the crowd. With the crowd there was money, and with money there was power, and with power there was safety. But this Jesus walks, if not runs, away from worldly power. He shuns it, as he did when the crowd offered him the kingship, and he walked away. Zacchaeus couldn't understand why Jesus walked away from worldly riches. Jesus didn't have a price tag, and Zacchaeus wanted to know why.

So he did what he had done his entire life: He ran ahead of everyone else. He climbed a sycamore tree. The climbing of the sycamore tree means two things: First, in Palestine the sycamore tree is the silly tree; it has a silly fruit. Saint Bonaventure explains the word "sycamore" comes from *syko* meaning "fig tree" and *moros* meaning "foolish."[3] The fruit of this tree, small

---

2. Saint Bonaventure, *Commentary on the Gospel of Saint Luke*, 1792.
3. Ibid., 1795.

and bland to the taste, seems to carry no value. Zacchaeus, in order to see Jesus, must first identify with what is silly and foolish.[4] Second, Zacchaeus climbs up the tree, that is, he *ascends by faith*, to see Jesus. In climbing the sycamore tree, Zacchaeus looks silly. The world laughs at the Christian. Saint Bonaventure notes that faith is often considered foolish by the world, by the crowd (see 1 Cor 1:23, 25; 3:18–19).[5] Zacchaeus has received the invitation to *see* Jesus. He now takes the step of faith.

Notice what happens. The Gospel account opened by saying that Jesus was *passing through* (see Lk 19:1) Jericho. Shortly after, it says that Jesus is about to *pass by* (see Lk 19:4) the place where Zacchaeus was. More is afoot than mere travel. The path Jesus takes leads him to pass by Zacchaeus and by us. Something stirs in Zacchaeus as Jesus is about to pass by. So too something stirs in us, every day, perhaps just as it did in Zacchaeus. We may have turned away from this stirring, dismissing it time and again. Zacchaeus, even with all his difficulties, responded. He did not let his mistakes weigh him down. He can inspire us as well because he knows what to do as Jesus passes by. And for some reason, on this day in the Gospel, the presence of Jesus reaches through the din of the crowd, through all of the glitter and shine of the riches and all of the name-dropping and high-class attention, and captures the attention of Zacchaeus.

Zacchaeus climbs the tree and *ascends* above the crowd. Saint Augustine tells us that he actually climbs away from the crowd.[6] Zacchaeus ascends above all those people who said, "If you want to be something, if you want to make a name for

---

4. See Saint Cyril of Alexandria, *Commentary on Luke, Homily 127,* 505–506.

5. See Saint Bonaventure, *Commentary on the Gospel of Saint Luke,* 1795.

6. Saint Augustine, *Sermons (148–183),* in ed. J. E. Rotelle, *The Works of Saint Augustine: A Translation for the Twenty-First Century* (New York: New City Press, 1992) vol. III/5, 529–60.

yourself, you have to go out and never make a mistake . . . earn triple what your parents did in only half the time . . . or you will never amount to anything." He rises above it all. And he finally sees Jesus—and then something happens. Heaven does what it always does: Jesus walks past everyone else. He singles out Zacchaeus and says, "Zacchaeus, hurry and come down; for I must stay at your house today" (Lk 19:5).

How did Jesus know Zacchaeus's name? We have no indication that they ever met. Perhaps the Lord knew Zacchaeus by reputation, as many others did. Or, perhaps he knew his name another way. Saint Augustine tells us that Zacchaeus could welcome Jesus to his house because the Lord was already dwelling in the heart of Zacchaeus.[7]

Jesus says *it is necessary* that he stay at the house of Zacchaeus. The same word is used when Jesus says, "Was it not necessary that the Messiah should suffer these things and then enter into his glory?" (Lk 24:26). It is as if Jesus says to Zacchaeus, "It is necessary that I stay at your house if you are to be saved." Zacchaeus is floored—literally. He comes down from the tree. He descends in humility.[8] He descends to a different world, one that will no longer be dominated by the price tags and the crowd. He returns to a different earth than the one he left. Why? Because all the riches of heaven stood in front of Zacchaeus. Jesus singled out the one person the crowd hated and he said, I have to meet you and pour all of my love into you. The eternal action of the love of God stood in front of Zacchaeus. The love that was ancient before all time, the love that takes all it is and gives it all away, stood below the tree Zacchaeus had climbed and said, "It is necessary for me to love you . . . and no price tag is attached."

---

7. Ibid., 260–261.

8. See Saint Bonaventure, *Commentary on the Gospel of Saint Luke*, 1801.

Zacchaeus hurried down from the tree. And the crowd started to grumble, as if to say, "Lord, you cannot go to his house . . . we don't like him . . . he is a sinner . . . not him . . ."The crowd thrives on calling people names in the desperate hope that we will live down to our labels. But the Gospel says that Zacchaeus "stood his ground." He promises to give half his possessions to the poor. "Oh sure," the crowd can say, "even if he gives away half, he's still rich." But then Zacchaeus continues, "And if I have defrauded anyone, I pay it back fourfold." Zacchaeus gave only half to the poor, instead of more, for the sake of justice. He kept that half because he knew he had a lot more debts to pay, restoring fourfold to those he had defrauded.[9] After giving so much away, he would have had nothing left. Why did he do that? Because of guilt? No, he was simply imitating what God had done for him. Saint Jerome tells us that Zacchaeus, having met the Lord, gave away all his money and replaced it with the treasures of heaven.[10] Zacchaeus was free. We can be too.

Like Zacchaeus, so often, we can fall into the crowd. We often cannot see who we are looking for because of the crowd around us. We cannot see our son or daughter because we only see their grades. We cannot see our father or mother because we only see their net worth or their habits. We cannot see our family and friends because of the crowd: fashion, money, popularity all get in the way. We often make the mistake of building ourselves from the surface outward and then pretending from the surface *inward*, so that we will fit in with the crowd. We believe that our identity or worth comes only from the last thing we

---

9. See Saint Augustine, *Sermons (148–183)*, 260–261.

10. See Saint Jerome, *Homily on Psalm 83 (84)* in *Homilies on the Psalms (1–59)*, Fathers of the Church: A New Translation (Washington DC: The Catholic University of America Press, 1964), vol. 48, 119.

did well, or what we drive, what we wear, whom we know, what others think about us, or from the price tags.

Jesus told Zacchaeus to come down from the tree so that Jesus could ascend it on Calvary. Jesus went to the cross of Calvary so that everyone could see him. From that tree Jesus gives everything away, even to the last drop of his blood. That same eternal action of love is given in the Eucharist at every Mass.

In the Eucharist we glimpse Someone. He comes closer. He singles us out. In the Eucharist all the riches of heaven are opened before us. We have never seen anything like this before, and we stand tall with Zacchaeus, who had never seen anyone like Jesus before.

CHAPTER TWELVE

The Pool of Bethesda

After this there was a festival of the Jews, and Jesus went up to Jerusalem. Now in Jerusalem by the Sheep Gate there is a pool, called in Hebrew Beth-zatha, which has five porticoes. In these lay many invalids—blind, lame, and paralyzed waiting for the stirring of the water. For an angel of the Lord went down at certain seasons into the pool; and stirred up the water; whoever stepped in first after the stirring of the water was made well from whatever disease that person had. One man was there who had been ill for thirty-eight years. When Jesus saw him lying there and knew that he had been there a long time, he said to him, "Do you want to be made well?" The sick man answered him, "Sir, I have no one to put me into the pool when the water is stirred up; and while I am making my way, someone else steps down ahead of me." Jesus said to him, "Stand up, take your mat and walk." At once the man was made well, and he took up his mat and began to walk. (Jn 5:1–9)

W e are never prepared to hear someone say the word "cancer." When we do hear it, our next word is likely to be a
prayer for the person who received the painful diagnosis. We
pray instantly and insistently that those we love will recover
rapidly. Prayer for healing is perhaps the most frequent and
energetic prayer we offer. We pray for emotional healing, for
the healing of memories and of wounded relationships, or for
help to overcome addictions.

Sometimes when we hear a Gospel account of Jesus healing
the sick, we may think: it's so easy for Jesus to heal, so why
doesn't he heal our loved ones? We may even wish that we or
our friends and loved ones could trade places with the sick person in the Gospel and be fully healed. Then the cancer would go
away, the depression or anxiety would lift, and the sick child
would be well again—immediately.

And so we come to the pool of Bethesda. It may seem that
this Gospel presents only three simple steps to healing: First,
the man meets Jesus, then the man asks Jesus to heal him, and
finally Jesus heals him right away. So the question returns: Why
can't it be that way for us? The Gospel makes it all seem so
simple.

Yet, when Jesus heals, more happens than what first meets
the eye. Besides the three simple steps, the passage records three
other aspects of this healing. These things are noted at the beginning of this passage and set the scene for the healing: First,
Jesus "went up to Jerusalem" (Jn 5:1); second, there is a pool
there (see Jn 5:2); third, there were *many* by the pool who were
"blind, lame, and paralyzed" (Jn 5:3).

The fact that Jesus "went up" to Jerusalem *appears* to be an
incidental geographic detail, hardly worth mentioning. But, as
often happens with the Lord, when we look more closely, we see
much more. The Greek word translated as "went up" *anebē*, is a
form of *anabainō*, which means "to ascend." It is used of Jesus

several times in the Gospel, for example, at his baptism: "And when Jesus had been baptized, just as he came up from the water, suddenly the heavens were opened to him and he saw the Spirit of God descending like a dove and alighting on him" (Mt 3:16, Mk 1:10). Jesus also "goes up" (*anabainō*) the mountain to call the apostles (see Mk 3:13), to teach (see Mt 5:1, Jn 7:14), to heal (see Mt 15:29), to pray prior to the miracle of the calming of the storm and sea (see Mt 14:23; Mk 6:46), to pray prior to the transfiguration (see Lk 9:28). Even at the age of twelve, Jesus "goes up" (*anabainō*) to Jerusalem and is found teaching in the temple precincts. The friends of the paralytic who carry the sick man to meet the Lord first "go up" (*anabainō*) to the roof of the house (see Lk 9:28) so that the man can descend into the presence of Jesus. Zacchaeus "went up" (*anabainō*) into the tree and then meets Jesus (see Lk 19:4). Most especially, the Lord "goes up" (*anabainō*) to Jerusalem to suffer his sacred passion (see Mt 20:17–18; Mk 10:32–33; Lk 18:31, 19:28).

The ascent and descent are two central actions in prayer and our relationship with God. As the Lord is baptized, for example, we see the larger action that takes place. The descent of the Son under the waters, his self-emptying, is part of a larger action within God: as the Son ascends from the self-emptying, the going under the waters, the Father descends and sends the Holy Spirit. These are all part of the one action of divine love. This happens in our baptism as well. Our "going up," the *anabasis*, is our response to God's prior invitation, to his pouring out of himself in love.

Before every action of Jesus this first mysterious "going up," this "ascent," occurs, which is, in essence, his turning to the Father. And this turning, from all eternity, brings forth and summons the action of the Holy Spirit. The sacraments, prayer, works of mercy, all begin with our turning toward the Father, in the posture of Jesus, formed by the Holy Spirit.

So too, on this day, as Jesus approaches the pool of Bethesda, he "goes up." He ascends, he turns to the Father, and the action of the Holy Spirit pours forth. In this movement of Jesus, the Son always turns toward the Father in the love of the Holy Spirit. So Jesus arrives at the pool of Bethesda, which means "house of mercy." The Son is drawn to the place of mercy. This is the second event or circumstance that sets the scene for the healing Jesus performs. The pool mentioned here (*kolymbēthra*) does not mean a swimming pool, but rather implies an action: it is "a place for diving." Notice Jesus has "gone up" to Jerusalem and now he has come to the place of mercy, the place of descent, the place of diving into the depths.

And so, in this place of mercy Jesus meets the "large number" of people who are ill. Jesus has "gone up" to Jerusalem on a feast. Yet, it appears that on this feast many cannot share in the joy. They gather near the five porticoes at the pool of Bethesda. This is the third happening or event that sets the scene for the passage. Saint John emphasizes that many people crowded into this large place. The five doors remind us that we can enter into pain and illness in life in many different ways. The Gospel tells us that "many" (Jn 5:3) gathered; the house of mercy was *exceedingly full* of those who were extraordinarily broken and in exceptional pain. It is ironic that in the place dedicated to healing, so many still needed it.

And none of those present that day wanted to be there.

Except One.

Jesus always seeks out the lowliest and forgotten. It is as if he is naturally attracted to the last place. Jesus walks among them there, among the ill, who are referred to as *astheneia*. This word means those who are weak, feeble, needy, poor, and powerless. Jesus also meets the blind and the lame. All of these people are also cut off, segregated to this place where the source of healing is rationed and meager.

They all have one thing in common: they are all waiting for the stirring of the water. Waiting, in Greek *ekdechomai*, means "to receive" or "to accept," and is literally based on the gesture of acceptance as a "holding by the hand." In a sense the word for healing means the favorable reception, sustaining embrace and endurance of friendship . . . to hold the hand of the other. Those who sit by the pool are waiting for the healing that comes forth from the reception of love, from the communion of authentic charity.

The Gospel next tells us that "one man was there" (Jn 5:5). We do not learn his name. He remains anonymous. He is, in a sense, every person of every time and place who needs healing. He is every sinner who needs forgiveness. We learn he is ill, weak, and infirm, and has been for *thirty-eight years*. Saint John explains, "One man was there who had been ill for thirty-eight years" (Jn 5:5). Imagine what it was like for him. Imagine the weight of the sickness multiplied by the long wait for healing.

It is easy to want to trade places with that anonymous man on the day he was healed. But few would want to trade places with him in the first year of his illness, or in the fourth, eighth, or seventeenth year. Even after lying there ill for nearly two generations, it appears he has not given up hope. Hope, like this man, *remains*.

Besides the Lord another is attracted to this place: the angel who stirs the waters. "For an angel of the Lord went down at certain seasons into the pool; and stirred up the water; whoever stepped in first after the stirring of the water was made well from whatever disease that person had" (Jn 5:4). The angel dives or "goes down" (*katebainen*) into the waters. A mysterious two-fold movement occurs: Jesus "goes up" to Jerusalem, and the angel "goes down" into the water. Recall that it was the descent/ascent of the Lord into the waters of baptism that occasioned the sky opening up and the descent of the Holy Spirit. On a larger scale, the loving, eternal exchange between the Father and the Son, the descent and ascent of their love, that is, the Holy Spirit, stirs the waters. More, he is both the water and the stirring. His action is always summoned by the Son turning toward the Father.

We are told that the angel goes down in a "certain season" or "from time to time" into the water. The Greek word used here for "time" is *kairos*, which means the opportune, appointed, and decisive time one has awaited. This sense of time is not the measurable time that we know by a clock's ticking. This is time in its immeasurable and supreme sense, a time that is so filled with joy that we don't even notice it passing. Notice the difference in the way time is mentioned in the passage. The angel goes down into the pool and stirs the waters at the opportune or appointed time (*kairos*). This refers to *the time of Christ*: the immeasurable, ever-present, favorable now, the time of blessing that passes in such a way that we hardly notice. The sick man has been there, on the other hand, "a long time"—*chronos*. *Chronos* refers to the measured and itemized time that passes and slips away to become lost in the past, finally closing off possibility. As Jesus "goes up" to Jerusalem on this feast, the *kairos* of the Lord, the time of salvation, is about to meet the *chronos* of the world: those who are marginalized and cast aside. According to the ways of the world, the weak and needy have been put in their place, and they had better stay put. Notice the contrast between the angel who arrives at the *kairos*, the appointed time, and this man who seems to have no opportune time, no appointed moment. All of his moments run together

When the angel stirs the waters, whoever arrives first is healed. The word for healed *hygiēs* means to restore so as to grow and increase, to become greater. This word can also refer to the interior growth of the Christian. Yet the healing is broad. The person is healed of "*whatsoever* sickness" (*dēpote nosēma*) he may have. *Dēpote* means "made, at last, exactly" as sound as the person was before the disease. So there is a great incentive to get to the pool first: whoever does so is healed of whatever ails him; all is made well, as all regrets vanish into the pool. But, even here, the pool that gives such broad healing has been co-opted—for the system of "healing" isolates: only the first make it. Many are left behind, to fend for themselves, just as this man has been left for thirty-eight years. How can a system that heals only one at a time, leaving so many behind, be one of mercy? This system hurts more than it helps, victimizes more than it frees.

Saint John explains, "Jesus saw him lying there and knew he had been ill for a long time" (Jn 5:6 NAB). How did Jesus know he had been ill for so long? Perhaps it was simply evident from his painful, infected wounds, his prominent scars, and his dirty, tattered clothes. The man explains the logistics of the situation to Jesus: "Sir, I have no one to put me into the pool when the water is stirred up; and while I am making my way, someone else steps down ahead of me" (Jn 5:7). Not only is he ill, but for two generations *he has failed*. Not only has his body failed him, but now his very illness also *prevents* his healing. He is too weak. Healing has become, like everything else, a race and a competition. And he falls behind to the collective last place.

But there, Someone new emerges. Not only does Jesus see the man, but the man sees Jesus and addresses him as "sir." Thirty-eight years has not destroyed his humility. He never gave up hope. Each time the water is stirred up he goes on his "way," to try one more time. Moreover, he tells Jesus the still deeper truth: "Sir, *I have no one* . . ." This is the deeper affliction, the distressing diagnosis that underlies and in some sense causes his illness: the system has protected itself by isolating the sick and the ill. The system for healing badly needed healing. Once the angel stirred the waters, human beings intervened and declared who would be the winner. The very ones who need mercy are cast out. But the Lord "goes up" to this isolated place. In the midst of isolation Jesus announces the great invitation. In the midst of division he will settle only for unity.

The man has told Jesus the reason, but without complaining or excusing himself. It is as if he has gone to confession to Jesus: "I have no one. . . ." Others always seemed to be quicker, closer, faster. Perhaps he often strategized on how to get to the source of healing. Maybe he attempted to time the surging of the pool, to predict the next healing moment. Maybe he had made a deal to help others who, once healed, turned their backs and abandoned him. Nothing worked. He was always at least a moment too late. But now he has told the One who is the Way. Jesus is the One who will go down into the waters of death in his sacred passion and crucifixion. On the cross, the Lord will take the place of this man and of every sinner in history. The Lord will be cast out to the margins, beaten, mocked, spat upon, tortured, crowned with thorns, and crucified. And then he will cross the margin of death. He dies and is buried. The system wanted him to stay put. But faithful love always rises and crosses even the most abysmal of margins.

The man has whispered his plight to Jesus. And now, with his word, Jesus reveals himself as the "way" to healing and draws forth a new measure of mercy in Bethesda, "the house of mercy." The word of the Lord is not vague or complicated but direct and abundant. Jesus not only fulfills the purpose of this place, but he literally overflows it: healing is no longer confined to a season, a moment, or to those who take first place. Definitive healing flows only from the Person of Jesus, from his Word: "Jesus said to him, 'Stand up, take your mat and walk'" (Jn 5:8).

Jesus commands three things: first, he tells the man to rise (*egeire*). This word is the same one used to describe the resurrection of Jesus on Easter morning (see Jn 21:14). It would seem that Jesus is not simply telling the man to stand up and be healed physically, but that this very healing flows from and is a sign of the future resurrection of Jesus.

Second, Jesus tells the man "take your mat" (Jn 5:8)—the one he had been lying on for years. It reminded him of his illness. For so long he had wanted nothing but to be free of it. But after his healing, the first thing he must do is to pick up that mat. The word for "take up" (*aron*) is the same word Jesus will use when he tells his disciples to take his yoke upon their shoulders (see Mt 11:29) and to take up their cross daily and follow him (see Lk 9:23; Mk 8:34; Mt 16:24). Healing is not given simply for the individual's benefit but as a sign of the power of the cross of Christ. Healing enables the one healed to be the sign and instrument of Christ to the world.

Finally, Jesus commands the man to walk (see Jn 5:8). In contrast to the man's slowness in getting to the pool, Saint John emphasizes that the word of Jesus has immediate effect: "At once the man was made well, and he took up his mat and began to walk" (Jn 5:9). The waters of the pool were narrow and limited, but the mercy of the word of Jesus is wide and immediate. The man responds in simple obedience. Notice that the obedience follows upon the wellness: the action of Jesus comes first and from this abundant source flows the man's obedience. Obedience is the response of the person who has met the Lord.

In bestowing healing, Jesus upsets the vague, stingy system of worldly fear, and man again discovers that God has "gone up," ascended, to the height of suffering and the cross, and descended to the depths of oblivion and death . . . all because God has come to look for man. And from those heights and depths God has arisen and saved man. And so this anonymous man who used to sit at the pool of Bethesda, the "house of mercy," has been healed of his physical illness. Yet, that is almost incidental. More has happened. He has learned that what he always wanted, the physical healing, is only a sign of a much deeper reality. Jesus uttered not just a word of healing, but a commission: arise. And now the man imitates the action of Jesus: He rises and by the word of Christ is conformed to Christ. The man has "arisen." Like Jesus he has "gone up," and now he no longer sits in the house of mercy; he walks, which is to say that he serves in the house of mercy and opens wide its doors.

Certainly we are never prepared to hear someone say the word "cancer." And just as surely, when we do hear this or some other word of painful suffering, our next word must always be one of prayer for healing.

Healing is not easy or simple, nor is it grand or presumptuous. It is something infinitely more: it is humble. It is as meek as holding a hand: the hand of the sick, the elderly, the child in the womb, the dying, the immigrant, the forgotten, the lonely, and the victim. As we stretch out our hands, we pray to be delivered from preoccupation with our own needs so that by the strength of Christ we may serve the needs of one another. As we do, we are invited into the saving movement of Jesus; we ascend with him to the moment of self-emptying, the cross, and of charity itself so that we might then dive deep into the waters of mercy that alone makes all things new.

Every prayer we utter for healing is forever linked to and expresses the deeper thirst that through salvation in Christ we might dwell forever in the many mansions of the one and eternal "house of mercy."

Chapter Thirteen

Martha and Mary

Now as they went on their way, he entered a certain village, where a woman named Martha welcomed him into her home. She had a sister named Mary, who sat at the Lord's feet and listened to what he was saying. But Martha was distracted by her many tasks; so she came to him and asked, "Lord, do you not care that my sister has left me to do all the work by myself? Tell her then to help me." But the Lord answered her, "Martha, Martha, you are worried and distracted by many things; there is need of only one thing. Mary has chosen the better part, which will not be taken away from her." (Lk 10:38–42)

Martha had been waiting for Jesus all day. She had begun to prepare the meal from the time she awakened. She had his favorite food on the menu. She kept looking out the window to see if he was walking down the road. When he did arrive, she was the one who met him at the door. Martha has the privilege and honor of welcoming the Lord into her home. Notice how Jesus moves in a certain direction. He goes forth from one town and enters another, where he is received. The description of his geographical course is significant, for every action of the Lord contains infinite meaning. The description of his route—his *going forth* from one town, his *entering* another, and his being *received*—reproduce in time and space a glimpse of what he does from all eternity. He is eternally begotten of the Father. The Son then gives himself in eternal love, in the Holy Spirit, back to the Father. He is eternally sent forth from the Father in the Holy Spirit. He gives himself in love to our hearts, and we receive him. From our hearts he goes forth and takes us to the Father in the action of the Holy Spirit in and through the sacramental life of the Church. In welcoming the Lord, Martha gives us an example for our worship and adoration of him at Sunday Mass, in the sacraments, in charity and prayer. He promises us, "if you hear my voice and open the door, I will come in to you and eat with you, and you with me" (Rev 3:20).

Jesus has entered and Martha has welcomed him. Mary, meanwhile, "*heard his word*." The text says that Mary "sat at the Lord's feet and listened to what he was saying" (Lk 10:39). These are the same feet that Satan, quoting Scripture, told the Lord would not be dashed against a stone (see Mt 4:6; Lk 4:11). These are the same feet that the synagogue leader fell before (see Lk 8:41), at which many sought healing (see Mt 15:30; Mk 7:25). These are the same feet that would be bathed with tears and anointed as a sign of repentance (see Lk 7:44–46). These are the same feet that would be nailed to the cross (see Lk 23:33; Mt 27:35; Mk 15:24; Jn 19:18). His word reaches her very heart so that she pours herself out in attentive love at his feet.

First, Martha welcomes Jesus. Now Mary welcomes his word. Martha serves the meal while Mary serves Jesus in adoration. And Martha will have her word. She has been driven and occupied, busy and distracted. Mary has been devoted to the work of contemplation and worship, seemingly disregarding what are otherwise important tasks. The vegetables are not the only things that have been steaming. Martha is rather burned up, and she raises a simmering complaint. The meal, almost prepared, can wait. A family squabble breaks out. Mary, her sister, has done nothing to help her. Martha has had enough. She has slammed a door or two already. She has given Mary a few hard glances and glares. She has put down a plate or two of hors d'oeuvres with slightly more force than necessary. The little hints and messages don't work. Mary hasn't moved a muscle. She is just sitting there listening to Jesus. "Sure," Martha thinks, "Let me do *all* the work. You just sit there and relax." Then, it all bubbles over. Martha gets angry . . . in public . . . in front of her guests . . . and her *Guest*.

Sometimes, in the midst of a family squabble, a guest will want to become invisible and disappear. But Jesus is at the center, in that same scene played a thousand times: a family argument at the dinner table. The argument can unsettle everyone, especially the guest. As voices grow louder, blood pressure rises, and angry words are exchanged, the guest feels all the more prominent and quite out of place. The warring factions raise their flags. Jesus is no stranger to sibling rivalry. After all, as the Word, the Second Person of the Blessed Trinity, he knew the dispute between Cain and Abel, the two brothers, one of whom became envious of the other and committed fratricide. And here it is they are at it again, two sisters, instead of two brothers, arguing with each other.

If Martha were alive today, she would be nominated for the "parishioner of the year award." She could do everything. She could plan and prepare the best gathering and make everyone feel at home. She could draw up the perfect guest list, send flawless invitations, and beautifully arrange the flowers. She would serve the tastiest meal cooked to perfection and served on time.

But for all her good intentions and despite her best efforts, *something* was missing. Martha had given up caring for Jesus and started caring for things. Mary, instead, cared for Jesus. In Mary, Martha begins to see what she must return to. The Gospel tells us Martha was "burdened" with many tasks. Her burden was not just busyness, but busyness *and perfectionism*. Yet it was *more . . .* She was burdened by *carrying around a mirror*. A mirror has no depth. Mirrors, subtly, reverse everything—they get everything backward. As we gaze onto their surface, mirrors turn everything about us around. It may all look the same, but it is not the same. A mirror can cut sharper than any knife. In fact, many people use a mirror to *dissect* themselves. People painfully search the mirror for anything about them that *does not fit*. And, unforgiving, they see it every day. People are upset both by what they see in the mirror and by what they *don't see*. Instead of *ourselves*, we see in the mirror *a criterion* that we must meet, and like Martha, when we are done burdening ourselves, we can easily shift the burden to others. Mirrors exhaust us.

That old sin arises quickly, that sneaky sin of vanity in which no matter how much we have done right, no matter how good we are, we start to daydream—we begin to fantasize about our own magnificence. We begin to plan a great future based on all our good points. It is not the good sort of taking stock of the gifts God has bestowed on us. It is, rather, the wishing to escape, a kind of daydreaming about my future in a way that denies the gift of the present. Such musings or fantasies often begin with those two terrible words "If only. . . ." "If only my parents had been richer." "If only I had done better in school." "If only I were more athletic." "If only my sister helped me with this meal and to prepare for our guest."

Martha saw her sister, Mary, through such a mirror. It was as if Martha said, "Why isn't Mary like me? Why isn't she rushing around getting the meal ready? Why doesn't she at least take care of the dessert or fix the salad? *Why isn't she like me?* In fact, why isn't the rest of the world *like me?*" And then after trying to fix Mary, Martha begins to try to fix *God*: "Lord, don't you care that my sister has left me all alone to do the household tasks?" Imagine the irony of asking the Son of God if he doesn't care!

But the mirror makes us see the entire world through our own filter, through ourselves alone. Martha is really saying, "Why doesn't Mary mirror me?" She is saying, "Don't you care that my sister is not like me?" Further, she is saying, "Why aren't *you*, *God*, like me?" "Make your plan fit into my mirror, or else you don't care like I do." "Why aren't you, God, created in my image?" That is why Martha is burdened. She sees everything slightly in reverse. She understands it through the filter of herself rather than the presence of God who is sitting right in front of her. If we drag our mirrors around long enough, we exhaust ourselves by trying to change other people and make them look like us. Somewhere along the line, Martha's interests became her cares, and her cares became her *troubles*, and her troubles burdened her and wore her out. It can be very tiring to attempt to change everyone else in the world every day.

Jesus takes the cruel mirror and turns it into a window. Mary looks through that window. It does not preoccupy her with herself but invites her to go beyond herself. Jesus says something very interesting: "Mary has chosen the better part, *and she shall not be deprived of it.*" Martha cannot find what she does have, but by divine decree, Mary cannot lose what she has, the better part. "She shall not be deprived of it." Everything else can be taken away or lost, but no power in this world can take away love. And therefore she will never be anxious. Yes, she may get upset at something else next week and fight the same battle. But she cannot lose it no matter what.

Each of us, in our own life, comes to a moment when we begin to sense our own faith as we see the world. We do not need to prove anything or perfect anything. We realize that being Catholic in the world is an incredible drama, one filled with Jesus. Mary is silent in the face of Martha's complaint. She does not raise a word of protest, saying that she has already done enough. She does not criticize Martha for "always" being in a bad mood. Instead, Mary continues to gaze on Jesus. Nothing is lost for Mary. She loses no ground because she has not entered the contest. And the Lord defends her. Notice, though, at the same time he reaches out to Martha and summons her deeper, calling her name not once, but twice: "Martha, Martha . . ." (Lk 10:41).

The voice of Jesus alone brings security and restores peace. We have our own predictable conflicts and complaints that can easily make us feel troubled even in the midst of our very familiar daily work, study and relationships. Jesus is the Guest who brings peace and invites us to our lasting home. He never tires of drawing our vision higher, so that we see more fully the lasting meaning and ultimate purpose of every moment.

Every Catholic church has a window, not just a stained glass window, but the tabernacle and also the altar. The sacrifice of the altar and the presence of the Lord Jesus in the tabernacle—that is the vision through which we view the world, and the vision that gives us the strength to live as a gift of self: "This is my body given for you. This is my blood shed for you" (see Lk 22:19; Mt 26:28). Jesus invites Mary and Martha, through different paths, to share in his gift of love. Jesus longs for us to accept his invitation to a deeper live a life of grace, in and through his Church. Maybe it is time to put down our mirror and allow Jesus to transform it into a window. And in that window he invites us to see faces that we have looked on for months or years: the face of a son or daughter, a brother or sister, a mother or father, a wife or husband, a coworker or a colleague. And we start to see them a little bit differently. We begin to see their originality and the depth in their eyes. And as we look we find something much more enchanting than any mirror.

That is what Mary found at the feet of Jesus. Only love turns the mirror into a window. Faith is the window by which the path becomes clear to us. Of all that Martha had prepared, only one thing is necessary. Jesus is the one who goes to prepare a place for us (see Jn 14:2–3) with this one necessary thing, which our heavenly Father knows about even before we ask him (see Mt 6:8).

Chapter Fourteen

The Woman Caught in Adultery

Early in the morning he came again to the temple. All the people came to him and he sat down and began to teach them. The scribes and the Pharisees brought a woman who had been caught in adultery; and making her stand before all of them, they said to him, "Teacher, this woman was caught in the very act of committing adultery. Now in the law Moses commanded us to stone such women. Now what do you say?" They said this to test him, so that they might have some charge to bring against him. Jesus bent down and wrote with his finger on the ground. When they kept on questioning him, he straightened up and said to them, "Let anyone among you who is without sin be the first to throw a stone at her." And once again he bent down and wrote on the ground. When they heard it, they went away, one by one, beginning with the elders; and Jesus was left alone with the woman standing before him. Jesus straightened up and said to her, "Woman, where are they? Has no one condemned you?" She said, "No one, sir." And Jesus said, "Neither do I condemn you. Go your way, and from now on do not sin again." (Jn 8:2–11)

Even first-year law students could have told you it was an open and shut case. The finest trial lawyer in the country couldn't have gotten her out of this one. "The scribes and the Pharisees brought a woman who had been caught in adultery; and making her stand before all of them, they said to him, 'Teacher, this woman was caught in the very act of committing adultery'" (Jn 8:3–4). She was caught *in flagrante delicto*: caught in the act. The scribes and Pharisees say so. They believe it, and they are the authorities. They have everything they need: a crime, a defendant, witnesses, accusers, a law, proof—and now all they needed was a judge, a trial, and a sentence. They chose as their courtroom the crowded and open temple precincts where Jesus was teaching: an open and shut case.

And so, the proceedings begin. Something different emerges, however. It seems there is Another, a second Defendant in the background yet to emerge. As is so often the case, the woman is placed "in the middle." The Greek word for "middle" is *mesō*, and can also mean "in the midst of; among." The tree of life, too, was in the "middle" of the Garden (see Gn 2:9). The fire flamed before Moses out of the "middle" of the burning bush (see Ex 3:2, 4). The children of Israel walk through the "middle" of the sea (see Ex 14:16, 22, 29). Jesus, will be crucified in the "middle," between two thieves (see Jn 19:18). The woman is placed "in the middle." The middle is a place of focus but also of tension and pressure. When we feel the weight and burden of being caught in the middle, it is often just then that God is preparing to act.

The middle is never far away. In fact, we can often feel as though we are "in the middle." Life begins to pile up. We feel caught between one parent and another in a painful divorce. We feel wedged between doing our job and getting along with colleagues, and often this can mean making compromises: simply to fit in the workplace we feel we have to join in the gossip, cursing, complaining, or worse. Or we may believe that God is acting in our life, but we feel trapped in the immovable middle between our past and our future. As with the woman caught in adultery, it is at such moments that Jesus longs to emerge, forgive, and lead us in a new direction we never dreamed possible.

Her accusers explain that the woman was caught in the very act of adultery. Jesus had been preaching about love of enemies and care for the weak. The Pharisees now present someone very weak. Maybe she believed that adultery was the only way she could survive or make a living. In any case, the Pharisees point out what the Law of Moses commands: "Now in the law Moses commanded us to stone such women. Now what do you say?" (Jn 8:5). The Law[1] clearly ordered stoning for such an act, the act she was caught in: an open and shut case. The first-year law students would barely have to open their briefcases on this one.

But the drama sharpens with those words put to Jesus, "Now what do you say?" (Jn 8:5). They seem to have no doubt about what to do next. So why do they go to Jesus? The woman is placed "in the middle," but their *real target* is Jesus: "They said this to test him, so that they might have some charge to bring against him" (Jn 8:6). In the words of the psalmist: "Those who seek my life lay their snares; those who seek to hurt me speak of ruin, and meditate treachery all day long" (Ps 38:12), and "They set a net for my steps . . . ; They dug a pit in my path" (Ps 57:6).

And, in all of this, they are using the woman—again. Many men have already used her. Now, her accusers again treat her as if she is disposable. What would Jesus do? Would he turn away from his own teaching on love in order to follow the Law of Moses? Or would Jesus reject the Law of Moses and—so they thought—incriminate himself? They want to cast stones not to

---

1. Lv 20:10 and Dt 22:22–29; see also Dt 13:9–10; Ezr 16:38–40; 23:45–48; and Dn 13.

fulfill the Law of Moses but because they have hearts of stone. They stone her first with their words and then with their actions, and now they want to throw actual stones at her. More, she is unimportant to them, as she has always been to men like them. They want to use her so they can accuse Jesus. They want "some charge to bring against" him. What is his crime? Quite simply, he doesn't fit in their categories. "To bring a charge against" translates the Greek word *katēgorein*. Its root word, *katēgoros*, means "accuser" and is the name that the rabbis used to describe the devil. The English word "category" also derives from this Greek root. Quite simply, they can't place Jesus in any category, so they attempt to force him, *accuse* him, one way or the other—to control and so neutralize Jesus. He is now on trial, and the woman becomes, yet again, an object, a tool, a means to an end. And Jesus steps into the middle.

In response, "Jesus bent down and wrote with his finger on the ground" (Jn 8:6). In their long discussions about what Jesus wrote, some scholars speculate that it was the sins of the accusers. The Gospels do not tell us. But before we would ever consider *what* he wrote, we must consider the action in itself. He bends down to the ground *not* to pick up stone, but, as in the action of Genesis, to *create*. Jesus wrote "on the ground with his finger," just as the finger of God *wrote into the earth*. The "finger of God" is a traditional reference to the Holy Spirit. In the creation account in Genesis, the finger of God, the Holy Spirit, moves over the surface of the earth (see Gn 1:2). The very law that the scribes and Pharisees have referred to, the Law of Moses, was given to him on Sinai after it was inscribed into the stone tablets by the finger of God (see Ex 31:18). God himself now writes on the ground with his finger. The psalmist tells us that the heavens are "the work of your [God's] fingers" (Ps 8:3). Elsewhere in the Gospel, Jesus will tell the disbelieving crowd, "But if it is by the finger of God that I cast out the demons, then the kingdom of God has come to you" (Lk 11:20; cf. Mt 12:28).

But the accusers persist and push: "When they kept on questioning him, he straightened up and said to them, 'Let anyone among you who is without sin be the first to throw a stone at her.' And once again he bent down and wrote on the ground" (Jn 8:7–8). The sentence is handed down and the penalty decreed. The first-year law students would find themselves in over their heads. And so do the Pharisees and scribes. The case is not open and shut at all. In fact, where others shut, Jesus opens (see Rv 3:7). And he creates, recreates, and writes anew. Perhaps Jesus writes because he has seen something else at work in this trial. How did the scribes and Pharisees all know where to find this woman? And where was her accomplice? One cannot commit the sin of adultery alone. But to the first question, maybe they knew her by more than reputation. Since they are using her now, perhaps they have used her before, in another fashion—not out here in the open light of the Temple area, but in another dark night of anonymity. Perhaps it was a one-time slip years ago, or maybe a more regular acquaintance. Maybe they needed to blame her for their own weakness. And then one day, they finally decided to throw her away. They waited to catch her in her sin. With the psalmist she can say, "Even now they lie in wait for my life; the mighty stir up strife against me" (Ps 59:3). Many men had used her, and now they are using her again. The words of the psalmist arise naturally: "They track me down; now they surround me. Rise up, O Lord, confront them, overthrow them! By your sword deliver my life from the wicked" (Ps 17:11, 13). In any case, the scene shifts quickly. The woman becomes the witness, the scribes and Pharisees the defendants, and Jesus the judge—who writes mercy into the world.

They see quickly that as they took aim at Jesus they involved something more, they have allowed something different into this makeshift courtroom. They have admitted new and unheard of evidence; they have introduced a new Witness, and the tables begin to turn. The shape of the earth itself is changing. The very hand of God is upon them.

"When they heard it, they went away, one by one, beginning with the elders" (Jn 8:9). They leave one by one. Why? Because of love. They must depart. The stones of punishment fall useless before the Rock of Ages. Jesus wrote a word of mercy, but the accusers hate mercy and love. They measure, but faithful love is immeasurable. They blame, but true love is blameless. They can only accuse, but true love is innocent. "Perfect loves casts out fear" (1 Jn 4:18). As already mentioned, the rabbis named the devil the "accuser" (*katēgoros*). The woman caught in adultery can say, in the words of Revelation: "The accuser . . . has been thrown down, who accuses them day and night before our God" (Rv 12:10).

Her accusers cannot look on the Word of Mercy, so they depart "one by one." The psalmist says, "How precious is your steadfast love, O God! . . . There the evildoers lie prostrate; they are thrust down, unable to rise" (Ps 36:7, 12) and, again, "He delivered me from my strong enemy . . . for they were too mighty for me . . . He brought me out into a broad place" (Ps 18:17, 19), and finally "How they are destroyed in a moment" (Ps 73:19). Evil cannot stand in the presence of mercy because evil has nothing in common with mercy. Evil always isolates and divides.

After they depart, the makeshift courtroom becomes a confessional: "Jesus was left alone with the woman standing before him" (Jn 8:9). He cross-examines the witness: "Woman, where are they? Has no one condemned you?" (Jn 8:10). Is he referring to the Pharisees and scribes, or to her *sins*? In either case, they are gone. Mercy has driven both away. At last, she has her opportunity to speak: "No one, sir" (Jn 8:11). Saint Augustine tells us that with the words "No one" the woman confesses her sin to Jesus, and with the word sir, translated "Lord" she confesses her faith in him.[2] Adrienne von Speyr points out that for the first time the woman is in the presence of a man who has never committed sin.[3] She has not met this manner of man before. The others used her, but this One has protected and forgiven her: "Neither do I condemn you. Go your way, and from now on do not sin again" (Jn 8:11). Just as the accusers left one by one, so too, have her sins. She is forgiven. She can proclaim with the psalmist: "He brought me out into a broad place; he delivered me, because he delighted in me" (Ps 18:19), and, again, "When my enemies turned back, they stumbled and perished before you . . . in the net that they hid has their own foot been caught" (Ps 9:3, 15).

When Jesus meets sin, he performs an act of creation: he moves his finger over the dust of the earth. Just as man was created from the dust of the ground (see Gn 2:7), so every act of the forgiveness of sins is an act of creation. The Son of God takes to the dust of the earth once again and breathes the breath of life: "Neither do I condemn you. Go your way, and from now on do not sin again" (Jn 8:11). In the Sacrament of Penance, he writes not in the earth, but he brushes away the dust and writes upon and recreates our very heart.

2. See Saint Augustine, *Sermons* (1–19) on the Old Testament, ed. J. E. Rotelle, *Works of Saint Augustine: A Translation for the Twenty-First Century* (New York: New City Press, 1995), vol. III/1, 350–351.

3. See Adrienne von Speyr, *John: The Discourses of Controversy* (San Francisco: Ignatius Press, 1993), 148.

CHAPTER FIFTEEN

"Love Your Enemies"

"But I say to you that listen, love your enemies, do good to those who hate you." (Lk 6:27)

Those are the three most difficult words in all Scripture: "Love your enemies" (Lk 6:27; see Mt 5:44). Of all the commandments, this one is the most difficult. "Well, Lord, don't you know who my enemies *are*? Don't you know what they have *done*? Maybe you haven't met them yet, but if you knew them the way I know them, they would be your enemies as well." "Love your enemies." It seems that Jesus has a lot to learn about the law of the jungle, or, for that matter, the workplace.

It seems like an enemy could be made in a split second: something goes wrong, someone crosses a line, and bad blood begins. But it takes time to create an enemy, a long time, and several ingredients. Making an enemy is one of the oldest recipes known to man. You only need to take some love and mix it with a perceived inability or unwillingness to love. Then add a demand that cannot be or is not met, let it grow, and measure the battle lines that extend in a million painful directions.

It all starts with being drawn to another person for some reason, perhaps an attraction or fascination. Such a relationship is built on a kind of love, not necessarily in the sexual sense, but in the sense of a friendship based on trust and agreement. This budding friendship is built on an initial sense that tells me this person is trustworthy. Without this attraction built on trust nothing will hold our initial attention. This is true even in business. If two former business partners now battle each other in a bitter feud, the conflict grows even more intense because it was rooted in their original relationship of trust. Oddly enough, then, the first ingredient of making an enemy is an attraction to that person; we might call it a low-level type of basic, generic love.

The second ingredient needed to make an enemy is a wound. Someone inflicts a wound right in the middle of the love, or the agreement, spoken or unspoken. The wound is the letdown, the refusal to go any further, the failure to meet an expectation. The wound is the unwillingness or inability to meet the demands of an ongoing call to love or relationship. When a call arises in me and I respond by making an agreement with another, and I live up to it but the other does not, then the stage is set to create an enemy. And, over time, many wounds create a series of scars, and, sooner or later, the scars create the hard surface of an ideology or a rough way of seeing everyday life. That's when the enemy has grown to maturity, for an ideology eventually becomes a weapon. An enemy is someone who has been hurt too much or too often and does not know the way to healing.

It may seem like we can create an enemy in an instant, after one infraction, one crossing of the line. After you spent the first spring weekend clearing weeds from your garden and planting new seeds, the neighbor walks his dog on it. In most homes, the moment a parent sets a curfew for a teenager, an enemy can easily arise. My neighbor takes my parking place after I spent forty minutes clearing the snow. Someone at work gets the promotion I wanted. One player tackles another with too much force. I get a grade in school that I think is too low. These moments can be the flashpoint that puts the final touches on making an enemy. But the enemy is created long before the skirmish, before the little—or not-so-little—battle that we think actually *creates* the enemy. It all takes time. When for a long time we have not felt loved, we tend to boil down the emptiness to our most recent encounter. An enemy is formed from love that turns desperate. Some battles are so emotionally charged that two people do not talk to each other for years. Enemies are contagious. When we have an enemy, sooner or later we want an army. The straw that breaks the camel's back seems more important than the entire field of hay.

Jesus invites us to another place. "Love your enemies." That goes against everything in us. He tells us to go back and love our enemies. Is it that Jesus just wants things quiet and orderly? Is it that Jesus simply wants us to keep it all inside and get along on the outside? Does he want us simply to grit our teeth, shake hands, and mumble "Good Morning"? If we think that, we have misjudged Jesus and misjudged love. He did not say "Be polite to your enemies" nor "Be nice to your enemies." He calls us to much more than politeness or being "nice." We could do that on our own. He calls us to love our enemies. When we love, we are like God. We must stand in the middle of our pain and see the deeper identity in the other: the identity that is deeper than the latest infraction, deeper than their walking on my garden, deeper than their dog barking and the grade I didn't like. Loving our enemies prevents us not only from falling into the same trap of wickedness into which they have fallen, but it also extends a bridge to them, by which they too can escape the snare.[1]

Jesus summons us to love our enemies because love is the only way to change an enemy. But Jesus is not some remote teacher or guru sitting above the clouds, whom the human race must approach for occasional advice by which to live. Jesus is not remote. He steps right into all the chaos and confusion. He has come among us. Saint Ambrose tells us that what the Lord commanded us in word, he also taught by example in his saving passion.[2] He did not only *say* give your tunic to whoever asks, he let his enemies *strip* his tunic from his body. Jesus did not only say, "Turn the other cheek," he let his enemies continuously buffet his cheek. He allowed all of the pain of the human race, all of the self-absorbed, self-seeking love to come upon him. He took every enemy we can ever imagine, and he absorbed it into himself, and that changed the course of history. In the darkest moment of history, Jesus loves. He summons us not simply to bury the hatchet but to destroy it. God wants to create something, or recreate something, between us and our enemy. He wants to fill the hard, bitter void and start again with love, to form a new beginning of goodness.

What enemy is on our top ten list this week? Our teacher, student, neighbor, son or daughter, brother or sister, boss or employee, coach or teammate? We must love our wounded enemy not with our own strength alone but with that of Christ, so that the wound is filled with new life. The wound

---

1. See Jean-Pierre Torrell, OP, *Christ and Spirituality in Saint Thomas Aquinas*, 53–55.

2. See Saint Ambrose, "The Prayer of Job and David," in *Seven Exegetical Works, Fathers of the Church: A New Translation* (Washington, DC: The Catholic University of America Press, 1972), vol. 65, 356.

becomes a sign of what is created anew from love. Saint Augustine teaches that patience before an enemy is more important than anything that an enemy can otherwise take from us.[3] As John Cassian explains, patience is the most effective medicine for the human heart.[4]

It takes a very long time to make an enemy: someone who needs a lot of love and comes up short. But it only takes a moment to glimpse love and begin to fill an old wound with new life. The wound becomes a passage, a place of creation. We must enter the wound, just as Saint Thomas did when he put his hand toward the wound of the Risen Jesus, and called out, "My Lord and my God" (Jn 20:28).

3. See Saint Augustine, *Letters, Volume 3 (131–164)* in *Fathers of the Church: A New Translation* (Washington, DC: The Catholic University of America Press, 1953), vol. 20, 45.

4. John Cassian, *The Conferences*, XII.VI.5; 441.

CHAPTER SIXTEEN

The Sinful Woman

One of the Pharisees asked Jesus to eat with him, and he went into the Pharisee's house and took his place at the table. And a woman in the city, who was a sinner, having learned that he was eating in the Pharisee's house, brought an alabaster jar of ointment. She stood behind him at his feet, weeping, and began to bathe his feet with her tears and to dry them with her hair. Then she continued kissing his feet and anointing them with the ointment. Now when the Pharisee who had invited him saw it, he said to himself, "If this man were a prophet, he would have known who and what kind of woman this is who is touching him—that she is a sinner." Jesus spoke up and said to him, "Simon, I have something to say to you." "Teacher," he replied, "speak." "A certain creditor had two debtors; one owed five hundred denarii, and the other fifty. When they could not pay, he canceled the debts for both of them. Now which of them will love him more?" Simon answered, "I suppose the one for whom he canceled the greater debt." And Jesus said to him, "You have judged rightly." Then turning toward the woman, he said to Simon, "Do you see this woman? I entered your house; you gave me no water for my feet, but she has bathed my feet with her tears and dried them with her hair. You gave me no kiss, but from the time I came in she has not stopped kissing my feet. You did not anoint my head with oil, but she has anointed my feet with ointment. Therefore, I tell you, her sins, which were many, have been forgiven; hence she has shown great love. But the one to whom little is forgiven, loves little." Then he said to her, "Your sins are forgiven." But those who were at the table with him began to say among themselves, "Who is this who even forgives sins?" And he said to the woman, "Your faith has saved you; go in peace." (Lk 7:36–50)

Word gets around. She learned he was at table in the Pharisee's house (see Lk 7:37). How quickly did it take for word to travel from the house of the Pharisee, across the street, through the town to where this "sinful woman" lived, as the Gospel describes her? More importantly, how would such a sinful woman *learn* what was taking place in the home of a Pharisee? Saint Bonaventure tells us that she had learned of the mercy of Jesus, and his mercy attracted her to him.[1] Word travels quickly. And so does this woman.

Evidently this sinful woman had more than a passing connection with the house of the Pharisee. Not only did she know her way to the house, but she entered easily and proceeded directly to the table. She showed up at the door where someone, somehow, *knew* her, and let her in, despite her negative reputation. As she made her way to the table no one stopped her or even asked for her invitation. She had connections in that house.

---

1. See Saint Bonaventure, *Commentary of the Gospel of Luke*, 629.

Perhaps she had been on the guest list before. Perhaps the Pharisee knew her better than he let on that particular evening.

Yet, something else is at work in the Pharisee. He has invited Jesus to his home, to his table. In a sense, with this invitation Simon has begun to pray. More, it is a sign of his search. It seems he deeply needs the Lord's mercy. Perhaps the sinful woman and the Pharisee are both attracted to the Lord for the same reason: his mercy. Jesus yields to the search, answers Simon's prayer, and joins him at table. Yet, the battle rages on in the Pharisee's heart. On the one hand, "sin is lurking at the door; its desire is for you, but you must master it" (Gn 4:7). On the other, "Listen! I am standing at the door, knocking; if you hear my voice and open the door, I will come in to you and eat with you, and you with me" (Rv 3:20). Saint Caesarius of Arles reminds us that two guests offer themselves at the door of our heart—the Lord and the adversary.[2] With God's help, we must welcome Our Lord and guard against the adversary.

The Pharisee begins to falter in his weakness. As the woman moves to touch Jesus, Simon "thinks to himself." He talks to himself. When the Pharisees encounter Jesus in the Gospel, they always begin to mumble to themselves, "to think to themselves." This is how they critique others. The Pharisee said to himself, "If this man were a prophet, he would have known who and what kind of woman this is who is touching him" (Lk 7:39). Simon moves to condemn both the woman and Jesus. The woman is not simply a sinner, but a *public* sinner. Yet, we must still ask, how does the Pharisee *know*? Perhaps he has heard from others in the town. Ironically, though Simon has not

---

2. See Saint Caesarius of Arles, *Sermons vol. 2* in *The Fathers of the Church* (Washington, DC: The Catholic University of America Press, 1964), 371.

invited the woman to the dinner, he knows more about her than about the Guest whom he has actually invited. Perhaps the Pharisee knows her by more than reputation. Perhaps she has visited there on another night when it was not so crowded, even frequently. The irony deepens. Simon's unspoken judgment, "If this man were a prophet, he would have known who and what kind of woman this is who is touching him" (Lk 7:39), is also the judgment of the woman, expressed now in her actions. She *knows* Jesus is a prophet and even more. That is why she has sought him out. He is the one man who can heal her and forgive her. She has come to the Lord not to hide her sin but to show her wounds.

The Pharisee has called out to the Lord and invited him to his home, but now begins to retreat, seeking safety in the labyrinth of his own thoughts and schemes. The woman's sin is publically known, but Simon's sin is not. It exists privately in his thoughts. He plays the mental chess game of "thinking to himself"; his every calculated move is a sign of ambition. In his mind he criticizes Jesus, who knows what Simon is thinking. Jesus knows this by his own divine power and also simply by the look on the Pharisee's face. The psalm says, "Does the one who shaped the ear not hear?" (Ps 94:9 NAB). The Lord is willing to chase after the Pharisee, to pursue him with the great invitation to love, even if this means entering the puzzled maze of his thinking. In revealing the Pharisee's thoughts to him, Jesus reveals himself as a prophet and more.

As a prophet, Jesus surely knows the painful and sinful history of this woman. Jesus addresses them both: he *turns* to the woman, yet he *speaks* to the Pharisee (see Lk 7:44). Jesus has become the host of this meal. And he is our host as well. That night Simon was worried about who was on the guest list, what his guests were expecting of him. Did he look smooth enough? Was everyone having a good time? Was he making a good impression? He places incredible expectations on himself. When they cannot take their own perfectionism, the Pharisees begin to place it on others. Their world is filled with expectations and shortcomings. They can never measure up, therefore no one around them can measure up. Even the Son of God seemed to fall short for this Pharisee. We too can be kidnapped away from things that really matter as our mind veers into the past or future. The Pharisee in us goes to our weakest spot: "What do people think about me? Do I fit in?" It all swirls in our mind as our expectations take us prisoner. Fear and anxiety are the work of the Pharisee.

Jesus turns to the woman but speaks to Simon the Pharisee: "Do you see this woman?" (Lk 7:44). The love of the woman needs no words, but Simon's hard heart does. On one level the response to Jesus's question is obvious: "Yes, everyone in the room sees her." But Jesus has asked the deeper question, "Do you *see* this woman? Do you see not just the outside, not just the appearance and the looks, not just the habits and the faults? Do you see her as something more than an object that you can use for your own pleasure? She has learned that I am here in your house, at your table. She has learned it and you have not, because you are kidnapped by all the cares of the day, by all the labels you put on other people and yourself. You are judging *her*, but what about *you*?"

It is as if Jesus is saying, "Do you *see* . . . *this* . . . *woman*? She has, by faith, hope, and love, by the forgiveness of her sins, become a sign to you." Then the Gospel says that the woman comes in and stands behind Jesus (see Lk 7:38). Standing behind someone else and not looking at the person directly shows reverence and respect toward the one seated. Moses hid his face from God because the light was too strong (see Ex 3:6, 33:18–23, 34:5–9). Moses could only see God's back. This is what the woman does in Simon's home. She comes up behind

Jesus in deference, because he is so much more. Then the woman bows down to his feet (see Lk 7:38).

Then she cries. In sorrow and in tears she pours forth everything not worthy of God. She has gotten caught up by the world. She has treated herself like an object, and allowed others to do the same. She has thrown herself away. She has sinned. Saint Bonaventure points out that her tears are the sign of her contrition, her sorrow of heart.[3] Now, her eyes, which have seen who Jesus is, release it all, but her tears proceed more from her heart than from her eyes. Every man who has hurt her, every rejection and use . . . she pours it all out on Jesus, on his body, over his feet. He will bear it all to the cross. All the wounds, anger, and fear come out. And then she wipes his feet with her hair. Sooner or later we have to get things out, the wounds, anger, and fear, all the things we have stored up. We have to confess the sin. She does, and her heart is made pure in the presence of the Lord.

Now only one person is at the table for her. Jesus, not the Pharisee, is the host. Jesus has issued the irrevocable and most pure invitation. He serves the nourishment that restores her health. The love of the Lord transforms her into that blessed servant, of whom Jesus will say later in this very Gospel: "Blessed are those slaves whom the master finds alert when he comes; truly I tell you, he will fasten his belt and have them sit down to eat, and he will come and serve them" (Lk 12:37).

Jesus asks us the same question, "Do you see this woman?" The Pharisee is so strict and unyielding that he cannot see *repentance*. Forgiveness is beyond his narrow vision. He wants everything and everyone else to measure up to his expectations. We, too, can fall into that all-too-comfortable trap. Our

---

3. See Saint Bonaventure, *Commentary of the Gospel of Luke*, 641.

expectations, the voice of the Pharisee within, can make us blind. The Pharisaic attitudes blind us.[4] We might complain about the quality of the music or the singing at Sunday Mass. Perhaps we complain that the homily is too long, or the acoustics are bad, or the children cry too loud, or someone else sits in the pew we want to sit in. "Do you see this woman?" Jesus asks us too this question because this is the woman who knows how to relate to him.

More than anyone else at table that evening, this woman, the uninvited guest with her reputation as a public sinner, did more than *learn* that Jesus was at table. She *perceived* the identity of Jesus *in hope*. She *recognized* Jesus *in faith*. She *understood* Jesus *in love*; she, the uninvited. Ironically, the Pharisee, the one who invited Jesus, has not yet learned it even as Jesus sits before him. Jesus addresses his word to the Pharisee, inviting him by name, "Simon, I have something to say to you" (Lk 7:40). Because of the woman's faith, the presence of Jesus was sufficient for her. Yet the Pharisee lacks such faith and requires a word.

The woman has become the example for the Pharisee, and for us. She clings to Jesus, who *knew* what sort of woman was reaching to touch him (see Lk 7:39). She was a sinner. So, too, was the Pharisee, and so are we. Jesus allowed the sinful woman to touch him so that he might heal her and forgive her sins. It takes us a long time to learn that Jesus is at table. First, we must get rid of our illusions. We must pour out the illusion that somehow if we just make enough money, meet the right people, or make ourselves and our family perfect, life will finally make sense. It won't. We have no secret formula to find happiness and freedom. The only way to find freedom is to let go of our illusions and sins, just as the sinful woman did. When she had

---

4. See Prosper Grech, *An Outline of New Testament Spirituality*, 44–45.

done this, she did not cease kissing the feet of Jesus with love. And once she has shown her great love, she anointed his feet as if to put a seal on her love.

We can go to Jesus too, for he is at table on the altar of our churches, waiting for us. He longs for us to enter, to come before him, to let go of the world's illusions. If we spread the word that he is at table, that word would get around. And our world would change.

CHAPTER SEVENTEEN

The Unjust Judge

Then Jesus told them a parable about their need to pray always and not to lose heart. He said, "In a certain city there was a judge who neither feared God nor had respect for people. In that city there was a widow who kept coming to him and saying, 'Grant me justice against my opponent.' For a while he refused; but later he said to himself, 'Though I have no fear of God and no respect for anyone, yet because this widow keeps bothering me, I will grant her justice, so that she may not wear me out by continually coming.'" And the Lord said, "Listen to what the unjust judge says. And will not God grant justice to his chosen ones who cry to him day and night? Will he delay long in helping them? I tell you, he will quickly grant justice to them. And yet, when the Son of Man comes, will he find faith on earth?" (Lk 18:1–8)

Jesus knew something was missing. The street wasn't the same, even though it *looked* the same. The usual crowd bustled along. The shop owners and the merchants, the same customers

173

and commuters passed by quickly, each doing his or her own errands. Some might have even been going to the synagogue. But the crowd wasn't the same. He could sense it in their eyes and in their posture, and he could almost *feel* it on the surface of his skin. As he walked among the people *he knew* something was missing.

And then he saw it. He saw *her*.

A widow was lumbering down the street. She seemed uncoordinated as she shuffled along, bumping into people and mumbling to herself. She was bent over. She would often bend down and pick things up and put them into the bags she always carried with her. And everyone who saw her got out of her way. In Jesus's time, the widow was disenfranchised. She didn't count. In losing her husband, she *lost* her means of fruitfulness and support. She had no voice and no one to care for her and defend her. Her inheritance was gone. This widow lived on the margins, evidently without children to support her. She most likely had no money and no one to talk to. So as she moved among the people they parted, separating like the Red Sea. The crowds opened up lest it all rub off: the loneliness, the hurt, the lack of security. She had no voice and didn't have a prayer, or so they all thought.

But Jesus, who teaches us the necessity of praying always, knew something *was missing*. The life that he speaks about, promises, and brings is far different from the all-too-common scene on this street. The life that he knows for all eternity is an embrace and an event of love: The Father gives all of his love in one eternal action to the Son. The Son, in that same eternal action, gives all of his love back to the Father in thanksgiving. And in this same eternal action the Holy Spirit is the eternal fruit and bond of their love. The eternal, never-ending love of the Triune God abounds in superabundant fruitfulness. Nothing is missing in God: there is no loneliness, no shuffling, no void, no lack, no fear. We can pray always because when we pray, God invites us, and we step into the eternal embrace of his love.

Jesus reaches out not only to find what is missing but to rescue the one who is lost. And this day he sensed that one was in danger of being written off and lost, and he searched *it* out: the lack and the fear. He searched *her* out. And he found her, as if to say, "This is the one I approve of. This is the one in whom God acts: the widow, the orphan (see Dt 14:28–29, 26:12–15; Ps 146:9), the disenfranchised, the one who stands at the margins." God's activity begins at the margins.[1]

We see it in the public ministry of Jesus. He met the widow of Naim as she was leaving the city to bury her only son (see Lk 7:11–16). Talk about double jeopardy: she has not only lost her husband, but her only son. Jesus reveals his life-giving spirit in raising the dead man to life, and then gives him back to his mother.[2] Jesus also saw the widow at the temple treasury who, after everyone else put in large sums, put in two copper coins—all she had to live on. Jesus notices not the large sums but the smallest offering. Jesus has a clear affection and preference for those on the margins. He simply can't stay away from them. For those on the margins, prayer is always earnest, new, and deep.

If Jesus were to look at our world today, at our family and society, what would he start to feel on the surface of his skin? What would he see as he looked out? What would he see is missing? Whom would he find on the margins? Would he see people whom we think don't have a prayer? Thirty thousand children die each day from hunger caused by lack of development, inflicted by greed fueled through corruption and

---

1. See Pontifical Biblical Commission, *The Bible and Morality: Biblical Roots of Christian Conduct* (Rome: Libreria Editrice Vaticana, 2008), 35.

2. See Hans Urs von Balthasar, *Theo-Drama: Theological Dramatic Theory V: The Last Act* (San Francisco: Ignatius Press, 1998), 343.

international debt. Education has become a system of unreachable perfection and of anxiety that is all too easy to reach. Jesus would see the immigrant, the refugee, and the victim of human trafficking. Jesus has forever linked himself with those who flee oppression: the neglected and abused child, especially the child in the womb. Jesus would see the person with mental illness and the person who makes us uneasy. Jesus takes us to the margins insistently, again and again. He does so without regard for any political party, ideology, or agenda. He takes us to the edge, to the outskirts, and says we must ensure that something new emerges in this place.

There are others who do not care for the margins, who do not care for life. The unjust judge in the Gospel is a very self-interested and very self-concerned person. He has worked hard to get where he is. And all along the path he has set up barriers to ensure no one will bother him. But who eventually gets through to him? The widow. She gets through to the unjust judge, *all the way from the margins*. Everyone else declared her to be on the outside. But she begins to transform even the unjust judge, the one who creates, measures, and enforces the margins.

Every day Jesus gives us the opportunity to transform the world through his strength. Very close to us, closer than we think, each of us has someone on the margins: the person who is pushed aside, the different, the outcast, and, according to the world, the disposable. We are charged now to draw them close, not simply to write a check, but to *meet* the disenfranchised person with our eyes. We are charged to shake the homeless person's hand, to feel the calluses, the grime, and the dirt. We must feel all that because Jesus did it for us. This is where love emerges. This is where prayer thrives, and we see, learn, and understand the necessity of praying always.

Jesus could feel something was different. In response, he did not set up a social program to somehow clean us up inside and out. He did infinitely more. He went to the cross. He took on himself our sin, pain, and anguish. He suffered, died, and rose again. Whatever fear, emptiness, or loneliness we find in our life, no matter where it came from, he has placed a seed of love in it. We do not need to fear it anymore. And we have a prayer. In fact, with Jesus we can pray always, even on the margins. The unjust judge, instead, does not sense anything different. He wants us to be afraid, to step away, and to mind our own business. Then we can make ourselves acceptable to the world, clean ourselves up on our own, and somehow pretend to be perfect. But Jesus steps past all that and walks first to the widow, and then to the cross.

On the cross he looks out at another widow: his mother. Tradition tells us that Mary's husband, Saint Joseph, had already died. When Jesus sees Mary, *he hands her the entire world*: "Woman, here is your son" (Jn 19:26). The words of the Magnificat return: "He has brought down the powerful from their thrones, and lifted up the lowly" (Lk 1:52). What society thinks is unfruitful, lonely, and marginalized, God declares vindicated, full of life, and a font of untold riches. As we receive the Eucharist, the most perfect of all prayers, we come to the same cross that the Blessed Mother stood beneath.

While an unparalleled moment of devotion, receiving the Eucharist can never simply be a private moment—it is a public action for all to see. It is an act of faith, hope, and love. If we come to the Eucharist, we must also stretch out our hands to the widow, the homeless, someone in need and pain. After we receive the Eucharist and before we receive it again, we must stretch our hands to defend in every instance and circumstance the inviolable dignity and the right to life of the child in the womb. We must stretch our hands out to the oppressed, the rejected, and the bullied. Then, Jesus will not just *feel* something is right or something *isn't* missing. Through the action of the

Holy Spirit, Jesus will be born in charity, create in faith, and redeem in hope. And from this action of the Holy Spirit the world, or at least our three feet of it, will be renewed and, when he comes, the Son will find faith on earth.

CHAPTER EIGHTEEN

The Defenseless God

Little children, I am with you only a little longer. You will look for me; and as I said to the Jews so now I say to you, "Where I am going, you cannot come." I give you a new commandment, that you love one another. Just as I have loved you, you also should love one another. By this everyone will know that you are my disciples, if you have love for one another." (Jn 13:33–35)

To the world, it may seem as if Jesus is always giving us one more thing to do. He says, "I give you a *new* . . ." And everyone waits for the next word. A new *what*? A new *place*? A new *job*? A new *friend*? No. "I give you a new commandment." He gives another *rule*? As if the first ten were not enough? We still don't have those down, but he gives us one more thing to do. Was this one forgotten? Why was it so important to hold this one until now? But, as is always the case with Jesus, more is at work.

To those unfamiliar with Christianity, it can seem like a burden. It can seem like a list of things that always has one more step, one more thing to do or even one more thing to feel guilty about. But more is at work.

Consider when Jesus spoke these words: Holy Thursday evening, the night of the Last Supper. He has just washed the apostles' feet. And Judas has just turned on his heel and walked out on him, on the way to betray the Lord. As the door closes behind Judas, Jesus turns to the apostles and gives them the new commandment: to love one another. Precisely at the moment when Jesus was abandoned by one he has called to follow him, a moment rife with duplicity and treachery, Jesus calls his Church to a new measure of love. He says, "Little children, I am with you only a little longer. You will look for me; and as I said to the Jews so now I say to you, 'Where I am going, you cannot come.' I give you a new commandment, that you love one another. Just as I have loved you, you also should love one another. By this everyone will know that you are my disciples, if you have love for one another" (Jn 13:33–35).

In this moment of loss, pain, and sorrow, Jesus uses the word "*new*." We focus on the word *commandment*, but focus instead on the word *new*. In saying "*new*," Jesus reaches into the very depths of our being and of existence itself. He is giving us *the command to be new*. He does this in a moment of such distress, rejection, and grief, that no moment of ours can ever be far from or immune to his newness of love. Every moment we spend throughout our day obeying the commandments opens up as *the way to otherwise undiscoverable newness*. New does not mean shiny, unused, or the opposite of old. Jesus gives a commandment just as he is about to undergo his crucifixion. Contrary to popular opinion, following the commandments certainly does *not* protect us in the world. In fact, breaking the commandments is the way to fit in with the crowd, to be popular and to get ahead. Following the commandments moves us to the very center of the world and of existence itself. Whatever looms before us next in life, Jesus is already present there.

In giving us the new commandment, which is so close to the Eucharist and the cross, God has placed directly in our path an event that interrupts the timeless tendency always at work in the world and in our hearts: to be so easily caught up in and preoccupied with ourselves. This new commandment opens a new way of life: to love one another. In giving this commandment precisely at the moment when Jesus had every reason to be angry, embittered, and fearful, he declares that every moment, every relationship, every beginning and every conclusion is forever invested with a depth, a hidden passage, which leads directly to the throne of God. Ordinary human existence is forever changed, sabotaged from the inside out, so that it can always be transformed into a path to God despite any difficulty. The world attempts to convince us there is no way to God, but only a way to ourselves, that the only way worth following is that of acclaim, personal reward, and getting ahead. Jesus, instead, declares the newness: no matter who we are or how distant from God we may feel, even the most hopeless sinner is now confronted with an event of love in which and by which God makes all things new. We can turn to God at any moment. The turn is a turn of love, and love always has the shape of sacrifice.

Sacrifice is not simply what we do with chocolate during Lent. No. Sacrifice is the very nature and heartbeat of love. Sacrifice is the love by which I give myself up for the other:

spouse, son, daughter, father, mother, friend, stranger, or enemy. I give myself not grudgingly, not simply out of duty or obligation. Love and sacrifice happen when both are inconvenient. I sacrifice because I have seen the face of God. This is the newness of love. The fact that we can love means we can create and offer the gift of self in the very next moment. For all of our attempts at it, God is still attempting to introduce us to love. Love means I give myself over and up—for this person, and thus move to God.

The only way to make sense of my life is to give it away as an authentic gift: this is what God does for us in the Eucharist. God is constantly searching our mind and heart to transform us, so that we might rediscover the beauty of such love and follow him. Then we are released from all the things we have talked ourselves into during life: the shortcuts, frustrations, and dead ends. The event of love in the sacrifice of Christ on the cross is so new it simply will never end. It always seems like there is one more thing. But with God that one more thing contains heaven. God gives us the new commandment because it is the way we become like him.

> After Jesus had spoken these words, he went out with his disciples across the Kidron valley to a place where there was a garden, which he and his disciples entered. Now Judas, who betrayed him, also knew the place, because Jesus often met there with his disciples. So Judas brought a detachment of soldiers together with police from the chief priests and the Pharisees, and they came there with lanterns and torches and weapons. Then Jesus, knowing all that was to happen to him, came forward and asked them, "Whom are you looking for?" They answered, "Jesus of Nazareth." Jesus replied, "I am he." Judas, who betrayed him, was standing with them. When Jesus said to them, "I am he," they stepped back and fell to the ground. Again he asked them, "Whom are you looking for?" And they said, "Jesus of Nazareth." Jesus answered, "I told

you that I am he. So if you are looking for me, let these men go." (Jn 18:1–8)

Why didn't he run away? Why didn't he hide himself and slip down a dark path in the garden to elude their grasp? Having visited this garden so many times, he knew it very well. He had also slipped away before, in the temple precincts: "So they picked up stones to throw at him, but Jesus hid himself and went out of the temple" (Jn 8:59). But not this time. Saint Bonaventure points out that although Jesus could have hidden and escaped, he instead went forth to freely *offer* himself.[1] He did not hide himself in *this* garden, the Garden of Gethsemane, because that is precisely what Adam did in *another* garden, the Garden of Eden. We hide; Jesus does not. In preaching he had compared the Kingdom of God to a mustard seed that is sown in a garden (see Lk 13:19) and becomes a great tree. Jesus is the seed of the kingdom, the fullness of the kingdom, and he will be led from this garden to the tree of life, the cross.

As Jesus enters the garden on Holy Thursday evening, he crosses the Kidron brook that runs through the Kidron valley. This action is significant on at least two points. First, Saint Thomas More notes that "Kidron" means "sadness" or "blackness."[2] Jesus has already begun the passing over the darkness of sin. Second, just as at the creation of the world, in the Garden of Eden "a stream would rise from the earth, and water the whole face of the ground" (Gn 2:6), so too a brook rises in the Garden of Gethsemane, where Jesus begins the new creation. He crosses over it. In fact, *Jesus himself* is the fountain that rises to water the earth's surface. From his side the spring that gives life to all will shortly burst forth in abundance (cf. Jn 19:34).

---

1. See Saint Bonaventure, *Commentary on the Gospel of Saint John*, 864.

2. Saint Thomas More, *The Sadness of Christ* (New Jersey: Scepter Press, 1993), 3.

Saint John tells us, "So Judas brought a detachment of soldiers together with police from the chief priests and the Pharisees, and they came there with lanterns and torches and weapons" (Jn 18:3). Treachery is never far from fear. To betray Jesus, Judas must gather soldiers and guards to pursue fishermen and a carpenter. The soldiers bring lanterns and torches to seek out the One who is the Light of the World (see Jn 8:12). It is as if the light fades and flickers out before the light of his glory. They bring weapons against the One who is the Prince of Peace. The weapons are more for their own sake than for his.

Jesus not only refuses to hide, but he *steps forward* to take our place, and he asks the band of soldiers, "Whom are you looking for?" He asked the apostles this question when they first came to him (see Jn 1:38). He will ask Saint Mary Magdalene the same question on Easter Sunday morning outside the empty tomb (see Jn 20:15).

The guards respond, "Jesus of Nazareth," and Jesus replies "I am he" (Jn 18:5). The guards immediately "stepped back and fell to the ground" (Jn 18:6). Jesus has revealed himself with the name reserved for God in the Old Testament, "I AM." Even the guards who seek to arrest him cannot withstand the divine splendor but retreat and fall to the ground before his glory. Saint Bonaventure emphasizes the point of Saint Augustine, that the Lord makes the fierce crowd retreat in a mere moment with only one word and with no weapon whatsoever.[3] Jesus again asks whom they are looking for, and they offer the same response. Jesus tells them, "I told you that I am he. So if you are looking for me, let these men go" (Jn 18:8). In the words of Jesus, we see the truth that lies at the basis of all of human existence: "you are looking for me . . ." Jesus tells even those who have come to take violent hold of him that he is the One. He is

---

3. See Saint Bonaventure, *Commentary on the Gospel of Saint John*, 865.

not just the One they search for in the nightly dispatch from the guard post. He is not just the One they search for to arrest. He is the *One they are looking for . . . and have been looking for their entire lives.*

The words of Jesus in this moment reveal the ultimate truth of existence: "You are looking for me." Jesus tells us this as well: every time we turn to pray; every time we are distracted in prayer; every time we are tempted to cut corners, lie, or steal; every time we feed the hungry, visit the sick, or forgive an enemy; every Sunday morning when we decide to go to Mass despite being tempted to play a round of golf instead. "You are looking for me." He does not slip away. He steps forward and leads us out of hiding, to the embrace of his forgiveness.

> "Do you think that I cannot appeal to my Father, and he will at once send me more than twelve legions of angels?" (Mt 26:53)

Even as the Lord allows the powers of darkness full reign, he stays and halts the advance of legions of angelic light. As the guards of the high priest and the Pharisees advance on the Lord, a parallel heavenly surge occurs. Three groups are now in the garden: the large crowd with "swords and clubs" (Mt 26:47), the apostles, and the twelve legions of angels (see Mt 26:53). Each group seeks the Lord, who stands at the center. Then, despite the Lord's restraint, one of his companions, whom Saint John identifies as Peter (see Jn 18:10), draws his sword and strikes the high priest's servant (see Mt 26:51). It seems so logical: "The sword, if not now, when?" The answer is clear: never. The large crowd that threatens the Lord may wield their swords, but the Lord's friend must sheath his sword. He who said he came to bring a sword (see Mt 10:34) and instructed his disciples to purchase one (see Lk 22:36), now firmly declares the time of the sword is over. In this, the Lord is still teaching them:

"For my thoughts are not your thoughts, nor are your ways my ways . . . For as the heavens are higher than the earth, so are my ways higher than your ways and my thoughts than your thoughts" (Is 55:8–9).

So too, Christians today often want to follow the world's game plan. If the enemy uses a certain move, or so the logic goes, that tactic is forever fair game. But the Lord reasons differently. It all seems so obvious: in taking up the sword, Peter resembles this violent crowd more than he resembles the Lord. Peter thought he had the solution, yet his action only proved impulsive, impotent, and disobedient. In contrast, the multitude of angels stands poised, powerful, and obedient. At a nod or partial glance from the Lord, they would spring into action. Yet Peter and the obedient angels, different in so many ways, both receive the same command. The Son renounces the "twelve legions of angels" (Mt 26:53) and countermands the heavenly court's endeavor to defend him (see Lk 22:51).[4] The contrast continues: The angels hover on the brink, poised, eager, and ready to rush forward to defend the Lord; the apostles step back, needing only the weakest excuse, until "all the disciples deserted him and fled" (Mt 26:56). At the divine deferral, the disappointed heavenly host stands down, the order suspended, the legion adjourned, with the meeting postponed to the end of time.

> Then Annas sent him bound to Caiaphas the high priest. (Jn 18:24)

Jesus has never struck or so much as raised his hand at anyone. Now, he is slapped by one of the temple guards (see Jn 18:22). Nevertheless, the soldiers bind the hands that healed

---

4. See Hans Urs von Balthasar, *Mysterium Paschale* (Michigan: Wm. B. Eerdmans Publishing Company, 1990), 117–118.

the sick, raised the dead, multiplied the loaves, made the blind to see, cast out demons, released the woman bound by Satan (see Lk 13:16), fed the hungry, touched the leper, and gave us the Eucharist. Even as God seeks to free man, man seeks to bind God. And God submits. Man now binds the very hands that formed him from the dust of the earth (see Gn 2:7), and spits upon the face that blew into his nostrils the breath of life (see Mt 26:67). The Gospels tell us that the demons could not be bound (see Mk 5:3–4), so much did they detest powerlessness, but even more, in no way can they stand to ever resemble the Lord. The One who has been sent by the Father from all eternity is now sent bound by Annas to Caiaphas in the darkness of night. At every turn, the betrayal, the arrest, the slap, the false accusations, the denial, the binding, the parading from one court to another, the Lord is pouring himself out more and more. He gathers and takes on himself all the sins of all human history. God surrenders to the extent that the rope that now binds him will shortly be replaced with burial garments (see Jn 19:40). There appears to be no bottom to the emptying forth; with each moment it only increases all the more.

"What is truth?" (Jn 18:38)

In the most meaningful courtroom trial in history, Pontius Pilate cross-examines Jesus. Pilate poses his final question, which should have been his first: "What is truth?"(Jn 18:38). Pilate asks the only One in all history who can answer the question "What is truth?" Jesus *is* truth in his very Person. He himself *is* the answer to Pilate's quest. Standing before Pilate, Jesus is revealed as the judge "before whom all falsehood melts away."[5] After asking the question, "What is truth?" Pilate does

---

5. Pope Benedict XVI, *Spe Salvi*, 47.

not wait to hear how Jesus answers. Pilate chooses to walk away from Jesus—to walk away from the Truth.[6]

Pilate has Jesus scourged (see Jn 19:1). Jesus had predicted the scourging as part of his passion (see Mt 20:19; Mk 10:34; Lk 18:33). The Lord is also crowned with thorns, clothed in purple, mocked, and struck repeatedly (see Jn 19:2–3). Pilate then shows Jesus to the crowd, saying, "Here is the man!" (Jn 19:5). Only moments ago, Pilate had mockingly asked Jesus, "What is truth?" (Jn 18:38), and then walked out without waiting for an answer. Now, the Answer stands before Pilate, and Pilate points the Answer out to the crowd, "Behold the man." It is Pilate's praetorium, but nothing happens unless Jesus is at the center. He who is wrapped with light as in a robe (see Ps 104:2) is now mockingly clothed in royal purple. The One at whose name "every knee should bend" (Phil 2:10) steps forward and stands before the crowd, before the world. The Lord Jesus, the only-begotten Son of God, the Second Person of the Blessed Trinity, the Word made flesh (see Jn 1:14) is scourged, crowned with thorns, and beaten. And now he steps forward at Pilate's cue. His precious blood drips onto the marble floor. And he forever changes time and space: all history up to that moment and going forward into the future; from the farthest galaxy to the deepest subatomic particle. Only in the mystery of the Word made flesh does the mystery of man take on light.[7] "Behold the man." The Creator stands before his creature, while the creature mocks the Creator. The pride, anger, and violence of the soldiers and the crowd highlight even more the extreme humility of the Lord of the Universe. He absorbs it all.

> And when they had crucified him, they divided his clothes among themselves by casting lots. (Mt 27:35)

---

6. See Cardinal Justin Rigali, *Red Mass Homily*, October 5, 2009.

7. See Vatican Council II, *Gaudium et Spes*, 22.

And they crucified him, and divided his clothes among them, casting lots to decide what each should take. (Mk 15:24)

When they came to the place that is called The Skull, they crucified Jesus there with the criminals, one on his right and one on his left. (Lk 23:33)

There they crucified him, and with him two others, one on either side, with Jesus between them. (Jn 19:18)

Only a few short words describe the crucifixion of Jesus.

The obedient self-surrender of the Son of God on the cross is the central moment of all of history. The crucified Son shows forth the overwhelming and inexhaustible magnitude of God's eternal and abundant Triune love.

When the soldiers had crucified Jesus, they took his clothes and divided them into four parts, one for each soldier. They also took his tunic; now the tunic was seamless, woven in one piece from the top. So they said to one another, "Let us not tear it, but cast lots for it to see who will get it." This was to fulfill what the scripture says, "They divided my clothes among themselves, and for my clothing they cast lots." (Jn 19: 23–24)

Gambling is the last vice that Our Lord looks upon before his death. They treat his tunic with more dignity than they treat his flesh: "Let us not tear it" (Jn 19:24). Only a few hours earlier the high priest had torn his own cloak (see Mk 14:63) at the words of Jesus. The tunic of Jesus is preserved, while in a few moments the veil of the temple will be rent as will the earth itself (see Mt 27:51; Mk 15:38; Lk 23:45). Man now steals and divides the clothing of the very One who made clothes for man after original sin (see Gn 3:21). These very clothes became white as light at the transfiguration (see Mt 17:2; Mk 9:3). The sacred garments that the sick sought to touch with secret reverence and devotion (see Mt 14:63; Mk 5:27–28, 6:56) are now traded roughly and examined for their worth. The swaddling clothes of Bethlehem are gone (see Lk 2:7). Jesus fulfills his own instruction: "From anyone who takes away your coat do not withhold even your shirt" (Lk 6:29). He who taught his disciples not to take two coats on the journey (see Mt 5:40; 10:10; Mk 6:9; Lk 9:3) now has not even one. He has gone even farther than what he told his disciples. And all the while the soldiers are unwittingly complicit in the execution and fulfillment of Scripture (see Jn 19:24).

> Then Jesus cried again with a loud voice and breathed his last. (Mt 27:50)

> Then Jesus gave a loud cry and breathed his last. (Mk 15:37)

> Then Jesus, crying with a loud voice, said, "Father, into your hands I commend my spirit." Having said this, he breathed his last. (Lk 23:46)

> When Jesus had received the wine, he said, "It is finished." Then he bowed his head and gave up his spirit. (Jn 19:30)

Something is heard in the Son's cry from the cross. We hear in this cry the Triune love of God for the world.[8] The deepest mystery of the ultimate, infinite, and eternal bond of communion in absolute love between Father, Son, and Holy Spirit, bursts forth for man in the cry of Jesus from the cross and echoes throughout all time and space. The Father's incomprehensible nearness to the Son is exalted despite the immense distance introduced by the sin of the world. In completely pure obedient love, without reserve or limit, the Son takes that sin on himself. Jesus, the One who is innocent beyond all measure, has been arrested, betrayed by one he had chosen, denied by those

---

8. See *CCC*, no. 2605; see also Hans Urs von Balthasar, *Theo-Drama V,* 262.

closest to him, falsely accused, spat upon, beaten, condemned, tortured, and killed in a shameful execution.

The Lord takes all the sin of the world on himself (see Rom 3:25; 1 Jn 2:2; 4:10). According to the *Catechism of the Catholic Church*, "All the troubles, for all time, of humanity enslaved by sin and death, all the petitions and intercessions of salvation history are summed up in this cry of the incarnate Word."[9] Balthasar emphasizes that in the crucified Christ the absolute emptiness and hollow futility of all sin of every time and place collide with the super-abundant eternal love of God.[10] Blessed Pope John Paul II teaches that the Lord, in his sacred passion, bears the weight of every sin, affliction, weakness, rejection, and pain, and, in full solidarity with sinful humanity experiences abandonment by God.[11] Yet, as Jesus proclaimed, "The Father and I are one" (Jn 10:30) and "Yet I am not alone because the Father is with me" (Jn 16:32).

The cross is the climax of the sacred passion and the supreme self-emptying love of the Son. The Son's cry of dereliction and abandonment from the cross is precisely the culmination of the profound and prayerful action in which the Son, persecuted in the moment of his defenseless, violent, and sacrificial death, lavishes the gift of the Holy Spirit back to the Father: "Then Jesus cried again with a loud voice and breathed his last" (Mt 27:50). Pope John Paul II explains that the Lord offers this perfect sacrifice by himself, and that the

---

9. *CCC*, no. 2606.

10. See Pope Benedict XVI, *Jesus of Nazareth Part Two, Holy Week*, Kindle Edition, chapter 6.2, Loc. 2064, 2066, 2074, 2971, 2980, 3074 of 4202; see also, Hans Urs von Balthasar, *The Glory of the Lord: A Theological Aesthetics VII: Theology: The New Covenant* (San Francisco: Ignatius Press, 1989), 85, 90, 207–211, 533.

11. See Pope John Paul II, *Jesus, Son and Savior: A Catechesis on the Creed, Volume II* (Boston: Pauline Books & Media, 1996), 471.

Holy Spirit acts so as to transform the Lord's suffering into redemptive love.[12] Precisely here the absolute and complete generosity of the Holy Spirit breaks in, pours forth on the world and embraces all things in a new beginning of goodness in human history.[13] And the Lord expresses this in his cry of dereliction from the cross: "Then Jesus gave a loud cry and breathed his last" (Mk 15:37). The Son "gave up his spirit" (Jn 19:30) to the Father and to the world.

In the sacrifice of the Son upon the cross, the tragic chaos, wickedness, and refusal of every sin, of every time and place, meet the highest revelation of the self-giving love of the Son's innermost glory. The cross of Jesus is the sign of salvation. This is the moment of obedient love that shows forth in powerlessness and divine self-emptying when the Son *dies out of love* (see Rom 8:32, 39; Jn 3:16). The *Catechism of the Catholic Church* points out, "At the very hour of darkness, the hour of the Prince of this world (see Jn 14:30), the sacrifice of Christ secretly becomes the source from which the forgiveness of our sins will pour forth inexhaustibly."[14] Thus, Saint Paul pleads to know nothing "except Jesus Christ, and him crucified" (1 Cor 2:2).

Christ is *with us* in every loss, oppression, and despair. In fact, since Christ is the fullness of life, his death *destroys* death: *Death is destroyed by death.* Christ conquers all. Moreover, through the sacred action of the victorious Christ, death itself is transformed into the source of new and supernatural life. The cross and resurrection of Jesus break forever the bonds of sin (see Rom 7:24–25; Jn 8:34–36) and death (see Rom 8:2). Jesus

---

12. See Pope John Paul II, *The Spirit Giver of Life and Love: A Catechesis on the Creed, vol. III* (Boston: Pauline Books & Media, 1996), 245, 247, and *Dominum et Vivificantem*, 40.

13. See Pope John Paul II, *Jesus, Son and Savior*, 313.

14. *CCC*, no. 1851.

invites us to share in his absolute victory: to follow him and to take up our cross (see Mk 8:34). Only in the mystery of Jesus Christ do we find that the moment of stark emptiness is forever transformed by the Son's sacrifice into the moment of everlasting resurrected glory.[15] The Lord shares this everlasting heritage with us in the life of the Church, in particular through the sacraments, especially the Holy Eucharist.

---

15. See Hans Urs von Balthasar, *Mysterium Paschale,* 68.

CHAPTER NINETEEN

The Stone Was Moved Away

Early on the first day of the week, while it was still dark, Mary Magdalene came to the tomb and saw that the stone had been removed from the tomb. So she ran and went to Simon Peter and the other disciple, the one whom Jesus loved, and said to them, "They have taken the Lord out of the tomb, and we do not know where they have laid him." Then Peter and the other disciple set out and went toward the tomb. The two were running together, but the other disciple outran Peter and reached the tomb first. He bent down to look in and saw the linen wrappings lying there, but he did not go in. Then Simon Peter came, following him, and went into the tomb. He saw the linen wrappings lying there, and the cloth that had been on Jesus' head, not lying with the linen wrappings but rolled up in a place by itself. Then the other disciple, who reached the tomb first, also went in, and he saw and believed; for as yet they did not understand the scripture, that he must rise from the dead. Then the disciples returned to their homes." (Jn 20:1–10)

It all seemed like a dead end just a few hours ago, and it was, literally. They couldn't sleep because of it. They had followed an itinerant preacher from Nazareth who had spoken of the kingdom of God. He had healed the blind. He multiplied the loaves and fish and turned water into wine. He had stood toe to toe with the Pharisees. When he taught, people listened. The apostles must have thought: "We left everything, our families and our work. And we made enemies. People saw us with him. Our names have probably been crossed off some guest lists and moved higher on some agitator lists. What are we going to do now?"

A lot of people couldn't sleep that morning. Besides James, John, Peter . . . there is Mary of Magdala. She gets up after a restless, fitful sleep, still in shock, hovering between depression and anger. She doesn't know whether to scream or to cry. Now she walks through the cold morning darkness, which grows warmer as the sun begins to rise. But as she hurries down the path she catches sight of something. This dead end. She notices something different about the tomb; it looks different from the way they left it yesterday. She walks faster, and she squints to see, then she says to herself, "It's open . . . it's open. That rock is moved, that boulder that required many men to move into place. The tomb we sealed shut yesterday is open." She turns and begins to run to call Peter and John. Still, her mind races more quickly than her feet: "They have taken him. Not only did they kill him, but now they have also taken his body." She finds Peter and John and says, "They have taken the Lord out of the tomb, and we do not know where they have laid him" (Jn 20:2). Startled, they get up from their own disappointments and run to the tomb.

It is absurd to run to a tomb. Surely, no one is going to *leave* a tomb, or so we think, so why would anyone *run* to a tomb? But on hearing the tomb was open, Saint Peter, the authority, the pope, runs there, and Saint John, the beloved, *outruns* him and arrives first. John doesn't go into the tomb but waits for Peter, since love waits for authority. And Peter rushes in, without caring that he would become unclean if he entered the tomb. He runs in to what other people think is a dirty, dark, and ugly place. Then John, the apostle of love, climbs down the steps and looks into the tomb, "and he saw and believed" (Jn 20:8). Love believes. John saw the stone moved away, and the only persons who *could have* moved it, the guards, would have been too afraid to even touch it. They were under pain of death to make sure it *didn't* move. The Jews would not have touched it because doing so would have made them ritually unclean.

Someone *else* touched it.

The risen Jesus certainly did not *need* to touch it. Later in the Gospel we see that with the qualities of his glorified body, he could go through locked doors. No stone could stand in his way. The risen Jesus did not *need* to touch it.[1]

But he touched it *for us*.[2] And by touching it he transformed the tomb in its entirety to be a sign and manifestation of his resurrection.[3] The tomb of Jesus, found empty that first Easter dawn, along with the testimony of the reliable witnesses who saw and touched the risen Jesus, serve to ground all the hope of the entire world: These are the credible signs that demonstrate the ancient foe—death—has been destroyed.[4] The stone rolled away becomes the benchmark that points to the Cornerstone:

---

1. See Bede the Venerable, *Homilies on the Gospels Book Two—Lent to the Dedication of the Church* (Michigan: Cistercian Publications, 1991), 90.

2. See the reflection on the *pro obis* (for us) in Hans Urs von Balthasar, *Theo-Drama V*, 333.

3. *CCC*, no. 640.

4. See Pope Benedict XVI, *Jesus of Nazareth Part Two, Holy Week*, Kindle Edition, chapter 6.2, loc. 3236 and 3239 of 4202; *The Church's Confession of Faith*, 169.

the risen Jesus (see 1 Pt 2:4–8). He touched the stone and moved it for us to show us that our own dead ends can open up and be transformed. The dead end might be an addiction, divorce, disease, death of a loved one, or any trial we have to endure. Today marks the moment when the worst dead end ever is forever changed *from the inside out* to an opening. And in the last place anything new would ever emerge, the tomb, a new creation bursts forth. Mary of Magdala saw, but thought the body had been stolen. Peter saw and did not know what to think. John, the beloved disciple, "saw and believed." Love brings a special faculty of intuition. Love sees the disaster and sees a path. The burial cloths: *folded up*. Why would anyone stealing a body leave the cloths? Why would one cloth be folded deliberately as if the One who folded it was taking his time mocking death, as if to say, "You have done your worst, death, and now I have done my best."

He is risen! The *Catechism of the Catholic Church* emphasizes that the resurrection of Jesus from the dead on Easter Sunday is "the crowning truth of our faith"[5]; it is "a real event, with manifestations that were historically verified."[6] In his resurrection, Jesus did not simply return to earthly life as Lazarus did (see Jn 11:44; 20:5–7). The historic event of the bodily resurrection of Jesus, "the same body that was tortured and crucified," is "at the very heart of the mystery of faith."[7] In the appearances of the risen Jesus, the apostles and others clearly recognize the Lord as they had known him in his life on earth, yet, at the same time he is also in a new mode of being; his real body

---

5. *CCC*, no. 638.

6. *CCC*, no. 639; see also Pope Benedict XVI, *Jesus of Nazareth Part Two, Holy Week*, Kindle Edition, Chapter 6.2, Loc. 3322, 3372, 3382, 3405, and 3469 of 4202.

7. *CCC*, no., 645, 647. See also Hans urs von Balthasar, *Theodrama V*, 52.

before them demonstrates the spiritualized, transfigured, and real existence of the glorified body.[8]

Scripture does not indicate that a human being witnessed the actual event of the resurrection itself. Who raised Jesus from the dead? The faithful love of God the Father raised Jesus from the dead. At the same time, Jesus attests, "For this reason the Father loves me, because I lay down my life in order to take it up again. No one takes it from me, but I lay it down of my own accord. I have power to lay it down, and I have power to take it up again. I have received this command from my Father" (Jn 10:17–18). This faithful love that Jesus had shared in his ministry with John the Beloved, that same love is now at work as Saint John stands in the tomb and *recognizes* the Father at work in the resurrection of Jesus. Love is the ingredient, the only ingredient that will take a dead end and transform it into an opening. A Presence began to move where no presence could move—in a tomb. In the Mass, the bread and wine become the same Presence that moved in that tomb. Something moves in the bread and wine *from the inside out*. What was the opening to death is now the opening to life. It is the first day of the week, the first day of the new creation. When we receive the Eucharist we are changed from the inside out, and we begin to see with the faculty of love. Whatever life, *or death*, throws at us is forever open to new life because God has gone to our darkest place—death and the grave—and changed it from the inside out.

A lot of people were awake in Jerusalem that morning, but One was more awake than all the others. He got up from where no one before or since has gotten up: the death slab. And he moved that stone so that you and I would hear the good news.

---

8. See *The Church's Confession of Faith*, 168–169.

Whatever stone sits in the middle of our life is not heavy enough to stop life. And if we look around we will see more than an open tomb and some burial cloths. We are going to see some-one who looks like a Gardener in a robe whiter than any we have ever seen. He is stooping over his flowers, and if we listen we can hear him singing.[9] In the Eucharist we receive him, and we join his song.

<hr>

9. See Miriam Pollard, OCSO, "Holy Saturday" as in *Neither Be Afraid and Other Poems* (San Francisco: Ignatius Press, 2000), 69.

Chapter Twenty

The Sea of Tiberius:
The Old Ways Are Never Far Away

After this, Jesus revealed himself again to his disciples at the Sea of Tiberias. He revealed himself in this way. Together were Simon Peter, Thomas called Didymus, Nathanael from Cana in Galilee, Zebedee's sons, and two others of his disciples. Simon Peter said to them, "I am going fishing." They said to him, "We also will come with you." So they went out and got into the boat, but that night they caught nothing. When it was already dawn, Jesus was standing on the shore; but the disciples did not realize that it was Jesus. Jesus said to them, "Children, have you caught anything to eat?" They answered him, "No." So he said to them, "Cast the net over the right side of the boat and you will find something." So they cast it, and were not able to pull it in because of the number of fish. So the disciple whom Jesus loved said to Peter, "It is the Lord." When Simon Peter heard that it was the Lord, he tucked in his garment, for he was lightly clad, and jumped into the sea. The other disciples came in the boat, for they were not far from shore, only about a hundred yards, dragging the net with the fish. When they climbed out on shore, they saw a charcoal fire with fish on it and bread. Jesus said to them, "Bring some of the fish you just caught." So

Simon Peter went over and dragged the net ashore full of one hundred fifty-three large fish. Even though there were so many, the net was not torn. Jesus said to them, "Come, have breakfast." And none of the disciples dared to ask him, "Who are you?" because they realized it was the Lord. Jesus came over and took the bread and gave it to them, and in like manner the fish. This was now the third time Jesus was revealed to his disciples after being raised from the dead. (Jn 21:1–14 NAB)

The old ways are never far away even for the apostles. And this was *after* Jesus had risen from the dead. In fact, the risen Lord had already appeared to them *twice*. Saint Thomas had reached out to touch the nail prints on the body of the risen Jesus. But still, Simon Peter announces that he is going fishing. They hadn't been fishing for three years, by some accounts. Fishing was the old way, what they did before they met the Lord, before he had called them to follow him. Simon Peter is going back to his old ways now because he wants to give up.

For over two weeks now they had locked themselves up in the room out of fear of the Pharisees and the Romans. Despite the two appearances of Jesus to them, they are afraid. Fear can be quite insistent and strong. It can be disabling. It is never to be underestimated. Fear sounds the retreat to the old patterns. Fear attracts the crowd, and the only thing the crowd can do is *go along*. Peter announces he is going back to fishing and the other six go along. Their life had changed. It seemed to be falling apart. The One they had believed in, the One for whom they had walked away from their livelihood and families, this One had been arrested, beaten, and crucified. Even though he had appeared to them twice now, they still could not emerge from their self-imposed exile. They were known to be his apostles and friends. They had nowhere to go, no money and no food. So they slipped back into their old ways. The apostles got into the boat in the darkness of night. When things get dark and we feel the bleakness of distress rising around us, we tend to go back to our old patterns. And the old patterns and sin only make the darkness darker.

... but that night they caught nothing. (Jn 21:3 NAB)

Even the old ways were not working. To their disappointment and grief at the death of Jesus they can now add defeat of another sort: failure. It seemed like a curse loomed over them. Seven veteran fishermen caught nothing, *not even one fish*. Then, in the midst of failure and defeat, "When it was already dawn, Jesus was standing on the shore; but the disciples did not realize that it was Jesus" (Jn 21:4 NAB). Notice what God does when we go back to the old ways. He does not send a storm nor appear in the boat. Jesus simply stands on the shore at dawn. But they fail *again*: they do not recognize him. They had lived with him for three years. They had seen him twice after he had risen. Still, from a distance of only one hundred yards, they do not recognize him. But, taken up into the mystery of Jesus, even our increasing failures are transformed.[1]

Sometimes we too do not recognize Jesus. We are in too much of a hurry, looking out only for ourselves. We expect him to be somewhere else, to do something else. We bury him with expectations and disguise him with platitudes. We enlist him in

---

1. See the meditation on this by Han Urs von Balthasar, *The Glory of the Lord I*, 470.

our own projects. In fear, we go back to the old ways, and we do not recognize him. Fear makes us think again about the rush— of ice cubes tumbling into the glass, of coins fed into slot machines, of the momentary pause before a round of gossip, of dialing in to the home shopping catalog. Fear pushes our buttons so that we think that "*this time* yelling will finally work." "This time getting the last word in will finally prove my point." "This time if I walk on eggshells Mom and Dad won't yell." "This time when I beat myself up for a mistake, the mistake will magically go away and never happen again." And we keep going back to the old ways.

But when we do go back, God gives us the *new*—always. He gives us not the *brand* new but the *ultimately* new. Death is the ultimate defeat. Jesus knows pain and suffering, he knows about death. He merely asks a question: "Jesus said to them, 'Children, have you caught anything to eat?' They answered him, 'No.' So he said to them, 'Cast the net over the right side of the boat and you will find something'" (Jn 21:5–6 NAB). He asks them if the old ways have worked. He asks them, in a sense, to *examine their conscience*. Has it worked? Have you found anything in all of this to fulfill you? Have you found anything to eat? In the same way, Jesus might ask us, today, some questions: Have you found meaning in a bottle? Have you found that name dropping lifts you up for very long? Have you found the gift of self through a wire to a computer? Have you found strength in bullying? Have you found friends in control and gossip? Have the old ways worked? Have you found popularity in being a know-it-all? We could answer just as the apostles did, with an honest and truthful: "No." Their response is like the renewal of the baptismal promises in which they reject the old ways. It is like Confession.

"So he said to them, 'Cast the net over the right side of the boat and you will find something'" (Jn 21:6 NAB). First, Confession . . . now, the penance. Once they have acknowledged their sin, they can again follow the Lord, even though they are not yet fully aware it is he. They have at long last acknowledged a measure of truth: " 'Children, have you caught anything to eat?' They answered him, 'No'" (Jn 21:5 NAB). They are finally obedient. The old ways are gone. Years ago, if a stranger had told them how to do their job, they would have scorned him, and perhaps even started a brawl. But once they admit their sin, they *hear* the Lord without knowing fully that it is him: "Cast the net over the right side of the boat, and you will find something." He does not tell them they will find a boatload of fish. They will find *something*. It is as if he were saying, "You have no idea of the abundance you will find if you follow my word."

> So they cast it, and were not able to pull it in because of the number of fish. (Jn 21:6 NAB)

Meanwhile, what was Jesus doing? "When it was already dawn, Jesus was standing on the shore; but the disciples did not realize that it was Jesus" (Jn 21:4). The scene is very similar to that of Easter morning: In Mark's Gospel the women came to the tomb when the sun had already risen, while in Luke's Gospel it was at dawn. Saint John maintains that it was "Early on the first day of the week, while it was still dark . . ." (Jn 20:1). Mary of Magdala saw Jesus there but did not know it was he (cf. Jn 20:14). Similarly, with the apostles on this shoreline, it is dawn, and they do not quite recognize Jesus. Saint John tells us that on Easter morning, "[T]hey did not understand the scripture, that he must rise (*anastēnai*) from the dead" (Jn 20:9). So too, with the appearance to the apostles on the shore of Tiberias, Jesus was standing (*estē*) on the shore. The word for "resurrection" and the word for "standing" come from the same root word. It is in this sense that the psalmist calls out, "Rise up, come to our help. Redeem us for the sake of your steadfast love" (Ps 44:26).

The apostles are coming to see the risen Lord in their midst. Jesus, the risen Lord is already present with the apostles in this night of defeat, just as he was after Good Friday and Holy Saturday. Death is the ultimate defeat, but Jesus, the Conqueror of sin and death, has come now to save them in their suffering. Christ conquers all in his saving passion, death, and resurrection.

All night long the veteran fisherman could catch no fish, but now they "were not able to pull it [the net] in because of the number of fish" (Jn 21:6 NAB). It was only *after* the word and *command* of the Lord that they could catch the fish. Their success depends on Jesus and his word. It is almost incidental that they have hauled in such a great catch of fish. Even still, all seven of them together cannot pull the net into the boat.

Something is changing.

Not all seven are giving it their utmost.

One is gazing to the shore with the net now limp in his hands. "So the disciple whom Jesus loved said to Peter, 'It is the Lord'" (Jn 21:7 NAB). The Beloved is the *first* to recognize the Lord.[2] Up until now they did not see love for fear. They did not see what love was attempting to show them. Then one, the Beloved, recognizes him, because "Perfect love casts out fear" (1 Jn 4:18). *Love recognizes love. Love awakens love.* In the light of the dawning of the risen Christ, the Beloved has come to complete faith.[3] Love recognizes the Lord, but it is authority, Saint Peter, who rushes to him. The other disciples manage to drag the net filled with fish (see Jn 21:8). On recognizing Jesus their

2. Pope Benedict XVI points out that the tradition has indicated Saint John, the son of Zebedee, as the beloved disciple and the author of the fourth Gospel, see *Verbum Domini*, 5; see also *Jesus of Nazareth: From the Baptism in the Jordan to the Transfiguration* (New York: Doubleday, 2007), 224.

3. See Ignace de La Potterie, *The Hour of Jesus: The Passion and the Resurrection of Jesus According to John* (New York: Alba House, 1989), 169.

strength grows, but they are still holding on to and dragging around the old ways. They are not ready yet to *let go* of the payload that brings the illusion of security. Only love and authority have turned completely to the Lord.

Jesus told the apostles they would find "something." When they listened to his word, "Cast the net over the right side of the boat, and you will find something," and obeyed, they found ultimately not the fish, but *him*. Then, he commanded, "'Bring some of the fish you just caught.' So Simon Peter went over and dragged the net ashore full of one hundred fifty-three large fish. Even though there were so many, the net was not torn" (Jn 21:10–11 NAB). When he recognizes it is Jesus, Peter can pull the net *all by himself* at the word of Jesus. Suddenly, under obedience to the Lord, Peter can easily lift the net that previously all seven found to be an unwieldy burden. Finally, Jesus serves them the fish: in and through him, they now have dominion over the old ways.

It is our unshakable faith that just as Jesus is truly risen from the dead; so too, after the righteous die, they will live forever with the risen Jesus, who will raise them up on the last day: "If the Spirit of him who raised Jesus from the dead dwells in you, he who raised Christ from the dead will give life to your mortal bodies also through his Spirit that dwells in you" (Rom 8:11).[4] Death does not have the last word. Jesus has soundly and completely defeated it. This truth of faith is *more true* than the fact that water freezes at 32 degrees Fahrenheit. It is *more true* than the fact that light travels at 186,000 miles per second. The resurrection of Jesus and the hope of our future resurrection is *more true* than the laws of physics. The mystery of salvation culminates in Jesus Christ, the Son of God and the

---

4. See *CCC*, no. 989.

Word made flesh, who saved us from sin and death by his redemptive death on the cross and his resurrection on the third day. The mystery of the salvation offered in Christ includes the resurrection of the body, of our body. The resurrection of the body is an essential teaching of the Catholic faith. How it will actually happen is beyond our knowledge, yet as we participate in the Eucharist we already receive a "foretaste" of the glory to be revealed.[5] Our life is not based on or measured by how every particular event or project turns out day to day. It is based on our clinging to Jesus Christ in his death and resurrection in and through the Church.

Even though we may have known Jesus for years, perhaps we do not always recognize him even though he is only a few feet away. We might be stuck in some old ways. The old ways must die, and the new person, transfigured by the saving action of Christ, must rise. The death of the old ways and the rising of the new ways are signs that point to the resurrection, and indeed gain their very strength from it. Even though we may have prayed often, we are still tempted to forget, to slip into the old patterns. However close the old ways may be, the new way of the risen Jesus *is even closer*.

---

5. See *CCC*, no. 1000.

CHAPTER TWENTY-ONE

Saint Stephen: The First Martyr

When they heard these things, they became enraged and ground their teeth at Stephen. But filled with the Holy Spirit, he gazed into heaven and saw the glory of God and Jesus standing at the right hand of God. "Look," he said, "I see the heavens opened and the Son of Man standing at the right hand of God!" But they covered their ears, and with a loud shout all rushed together against him. Then they dragged him out of the city and began to stone him; and the witnesses laid their coats at the feet of a young man named Saul. While they were stoning Stephen, he prayed, "Lord Jesus, receive my spirit." Then he knelt down and cried out in a loud voice, "Lord, do not hold this sin against them." When he had said this, he died. (Acts 7:54–60)

Two spirits are at work in the world, and they will inevitably meet. First, the thunderous action of the Holy Spirit is often at work, though we mistakenly believe it is very rare. Saint Stephen, the first martyr, proclaims to the crowd that he is so filled with the Holy Spirit that he sees heaven open, and "the Son of Man standing at the right hand of God." Stephen is filled with the Holy Spirit. Isn't this the goal of every believer? But the presence of God the Holy Spirit does not mean that suddenly everything will always work out for Stephen. What do the other people do when Stephen asserts the presence of the Holy Spirit? Their response shows us the spirit of the world.

They react in five specific ways, actions that attempt to break love. First, they cry out against him. Second, they cover their ears, and by so doing they resist the Holy Spirit.[1] They want to pretend that the kingdom does not extend that far, and the best way to pretend is to pretend not to hear. Third, they rush at him. Fourth, they drag him outside the city. Fifth, they throw stones at him until he dies. They kill him. The stones fly the minute they realize that Stephen is filled with the Holy Spirit. The two spirits clash. It should come as no surprise, but it often does. This puts in stark relief for us where we stand as Christians in the world. We mistakenly try to interpret our attendance at church, our prayer, our living a good life, our sacrifices, in terms of the world—success and achievement.

But it can never be that way. If we are connected with the Holy Spirit, we will not fit in. It simply won't work. The world always wants to push the Holy Spirit aside because another spirit is at work in the world. The Gospel clearly states who the ruler of this world is: Satan. Christ is very clear about that. So the Christian will inevitably clash with the world. If we do not come into conflict with it, something is wrong. To see Satan's disordered plan at work in the world, we simply have to read the headlines. Before long we will be very convinced that an intelligent evil force is at work in the world. The crowd around

---

1. See Prosper Grech, *Acts of the Apostles Explained*, 53.

Stephen cannot simply dismiss his words and his message as rhetoric because his words made too much sense. Rhetoric is safe, but authentic truth is the great risk that the world refuses to take. Such risk is a virtue.[2] The Christian is not at home in the world. We have a different Spirit in us. The Holy Spirit is always moving in our deepest places, urging and strengthening us to see the difference between the two.

Stephen looks up to heaven and sees God the Father and Jesus. We too are called to this vision that the world continually attempts to edge out, to fool us into believing that our real identity is in our successes, achievements, and the things the world promises us. But these never satisfy us. We cannot allow ourselves to be confused about this. The crowd around Stephen picks up stones because the world cannot bear to hear about the Holy Spirit. First, they cry out to cover the sound of love. But love is louder than their cries, so they cover their ears to block the sound of love. But that is not enough, so they drag love outside the city, and then they attempt to kill love.

Often enough we are at odds with authentic love in our lives, just as the world urges us to be. Despite our best efforts we forget that original vision of the Holy Spirit that slumbers within us. The Holy Spirit is the Spirit of love, the Person-Gift of love. No matter how much we have allowed the world's illusions to deceive us, love is still accessible to us. The Holy Spirit invites us to make a gift of self, to love. But the world tells us, "Don't even try." The world convinces us that in order to be important in someone else's eyes, we must be a perfect success, as the world defines it. In order to be accepted, we have to go back and somehow fix things that happened so

---

2. See Jean-Pierre Torrell, OP, *Christ and Spirituality in Saint Thomas Aquinas*, 43, and his *Saint Thomas Aquinas, vol. 2 Spiritual Master* (Washington, DC: The Catholic University of America Press, 2003), 270–273.

many years ago. We have to look and act the part, and be the best. The spirit of the world says to us, "You are so far behind you will never get ahead. Don't even try. Just give up." The world would have us believe that joy resides only on the other side of success after success, win after win, award after award. The world throws off the internal compass of our life. God is the original eternal Event of love at the basis of all that is. Love always and everywhere takes the form, not of an achievement, but of a gift of self.

Every day we face the difficult temptation to fit into the world and get along. The spirit of the world rushes in at every chance. The world wants to cover the sound of love, drag it away from us, and finally kill it—because love costs. It costs the world.

Love says that we are not condemned to the past. We can find the invitation to love right now, right next to us, *within us*. For Stephen, the two spirits come together. Stephen declares that he sees the Holy Spirit. Those who follow the spirit of the world declare, "We must kill him. The spirit of love is going to cost too much and pull us out of our comfortable world. We are afraid. The world will give us what we want. Let's kill him."

But look what happens to Stephen when the stones start to fly. When the crisis heightens and the crowd rushes in, ready to take off their cloaks so they can really wind up with the rocks, then Stephen *can access his own spirit*, precisely when the spirit of the world and the Holy Spirit clash. Stephen then says, "Lord Jesus, receive my spirit." When he could believe in love and still face the pressures of the world, something opened in him so that he could access his own spirit. And in this, something even more remarkable happens. In the midst of the persecution, Stephen is transformed. He gains access to his own spirit so he can *hand over his spirit*. In this, he is most perfectly conformed to Christ. Notice that the words of Jesus in his passion become the words of Stephen in his own moment of martyrdom: "Lord Jesus, receive my spirit" ("Father, into your hands I commend my spirit" Lk 23:46) and "Lord, do not hold this sin against them" ("Father, forgive them; for they do not know what they are doing" Lk 23:34).[3]

It can seem easy for us to go through the motions. We can leave our spirits on autopilot and just fall in line behind everyone else in the neighborhood, at work, and at church. We might do what everyone else is doing just a little bit harder, with a little more polish, so we get a little bit ahead . . . and then we find out it doesn't satisfy. So we try harder, and our hearts become harder, as hard as those stones they threw at Stephen. We need something that opens access to our spirit. If we appear to have "made it" in the world and all looks perfect, something is wrong, and we had better check things out. Usually a crisis must occur to give us access to our spirit. When the world does not make sense to us, it is actually a good sign. In a crisis we question, wonder, and look for the next firm place in our life that really will give us stability now, today. Only authentic love can drive out the spirit of the world, and only Jesus is the source of such love. The world says love is control, but Jesus says love is sacrifice. Jesus pours himself out in the Eucharist so that we will be healed and strengthened for the sacrifice of love. That is a remarkable thing in one's life, to be loved, to come to the place where we can break free of the spirit of the world. Don't be surprised if the rocks start to fly, and people cover their ears. For precisely then we will be

---

3. See Prosper Grech, *Acts of the Apostles Explained*, 49.

free—free enough that we can reach our hands, our arms, *ourselves* around our spirit, and give it away to the person next to us. When we do that, God intervenes, or rather *supervenes*, and we discover again the Gift that filled the vision of Saint Stephen, the first martyr: the living action of the Holy Spirit that always makes known the beauty of Jesus Christ. Filled with this vision, the words of Our Lady reach ever deeper into our heart: "*Do whatever he tells you*" (Jn 2:5 NAB).

The God Who Waits

It is easy to make mistakes about God. The most common mistake we make about God is that he is simply a lawgiver, a distant rule maker who can come close anytime he chooses in order to check up us. The idea that God's main job is to follow us around and check off our scorecard is as popular and wide-spread as it is misleading and off the mark. In fact, the modern overemphasis on this idea of God is a factor that fuels the post-modern mindset's dismissal and denial of God. Yet, ironically, if we examine our contemporary, automatic, and unreflected-upon notion of God, it is *we* and *not God* who are often the lawgivers. And we reserve our most strict and inhibiting laws for God himself. Our standard disobedience is not grounded in mere flagrant disregard for his rules, but it is rooted in our demand that he obey ours. We want God to obey the laws we set for him. Our greatest law for God is the law of demand.

Yes, it is easy to make mistakes about God. The Church prays Psalm 95 every morning. In this Psalm (95:10 NAB) God says of his people: "They do not know my ways." The problem is that *we think* we know God's ways. And so, we make mistakes about God. One prevalent mistake today is that we can so often slip into treating God not as Lord, but as a cosmic *Land Lord* who is there to meet our every request. It is as if we sit tapping our fingers on a table as we wait for God to snap his fingers to fulfill what we have defined as his first and only task: to restore balance and equilibrium to our lives. In fact, if we suddenly found ourselves in his unmistakable presence, we probably would recite our well-rehearsed list of what we want God to change about our life, our family, or the world.

Many of us *expect* things from God, either directly or indirectly, implicitly or explicitly. The moment life swings out of balance, when we lose control or cannot work out obstacles, we insist that God must summon a solution. If God meets our demand, we reward him with our belief and practice, but if he doesn't, we punish him by withholding it. If God does not "keep" the rules we give to him, then we believe we can dispense with the way of life that he gives to us. More so, if he consistently does not meet our many claims, we can even *ground* God: We confine him to Sunday and then, only to the church building, and for one hour, but no more.

Further, if God does not meet our expectations, we stop putting our demands on him and we *distribute* those demands to the people around us: our family, colleagues, friends, and even ourselves. We persistently try to fix ourselves by making demands of others. Instead of remaining steadfast and engaging in personal and professional relationships as they were meant to be, we drag our needs into these relationships. This strains our rapport with others and taxes our daily life. We begin to see others only through the lens of our fears. Yet, as the meditations in these pages have shown, our lives, no matter how complicated they may seem, are never beyond the reach of God's grace.

When we associate God only with "the rules," we miss the much-neglected yet full beauty of *whom* he has revealed himself to be, and the *encounter* to which he has invited us in the Church. Once we embrace the beauty of what we profess in the Creed, and meet this Beauty in the sacraments, *then* we have the strength, given by God's grace, to live the laws and the rules *out of love*, not out of mere obligation and duty.[1] Some make the common mistake of trying to say laws and rules that God gives us are simply man-made and do not belong in religion. Such assertions could not be more wrong. We do not seek to do away with the laws and rules. As the Lord testifies, "Do not think that I have come to abolish the law or the prophets; I have come not to abolish but to fulfill. For truly I tell you, until heaven and earth pass away, not one letter, not one stroke of a letter, will pass from the law until all is accomplished" (Mt 5:17–18). Rather than getting rid of rules, we seek to understand them in their proper light. God does not issue commandments and laws in order to control and coerce us. Instead, *we* often want to control God. Rather, every command or law God has ever given is always first based in his merciful covenant of love (see Dn 9:4).[2] When we glimpse his mercy and love, we have found the moment of conversion, which can happen any time at God's initiative. We often only permit that moment into our heart when we are finally exhausted with attempting to control life and make the world work according to our stubborn designs. Love is patient, so it waits.

Our world finds it oddly convenient to condense God, to tame him and confine him, to shrink him down to our size. And we do that mainly by saddling him with our catalog of requests

---

1. See Servais Pinckaers, OP, *Morality: The Catholic View* (South Bend, IN: Saint Augustine's Press, 2001); see also his *Sources of Christian Ethics,* and Livio Melina, *Building a Culture of the Family: The Language of Love* (Staten Island, NY: Alba House, 2011).

2. See Pontifical Biblical Commission, *The Bible and Morality: Biblical Roots of Christian Conduct.*

that, over time, seem more and more to ferment into demands. We make many more rules for God than God does for us, and we enforce them to the letter.

Our requests and demands emerge over time from those recurrent disappointing moments or events that dissatisfy us which we mentally, almost unconsciously, point out again and again to ourselves. You know the things. Every Monday morning we pick up the mental checklist and chip away at it through the week: from one appointment to the next, from one meeting to the next, from one job *or job interview* to the next. Then, we face times of even more intense stress as we await a doctor's call about a loved one's medical tests. We can so quickly and easily go from a frantic pace to a fussed and frenzied hurry until we are simply fragmented, going in a dozen directions at once. We find it impossible to keep up or even to catch up. All the while we text our friends who seem to be even busier but have it all well in hand. Sure, they run along just as we do, only their busy looks *easy.* Our busy looks anxious and edgy. They seem not only to have it all but *to have it all together.*

As we survey all of this from Monday to Thursday, an odd thing begins to happen. We realize in moments of clarity that the more we *chip away* at the mental checklists, the *bigger* each list seems to grow. Finally, on Friday, with relief we put the lists down and glide into the weekend. Yet, almost unaware, one could say "automatically," we *pick up* the *weekend* list: more practices, rehearsals, and games, with dances and parties added to the mix.

Inevitably, minutes or hours later, worry's handyman, *regret,* shows up right on schedule. *Why did we yell earlier today? Why did we rush and argue?* Later, we even regret the worry. Externally tired, we are also internally exhausted. It takes *even more* energy to *hide the exhaustion* from others. Tomorrow will be different. On Sunday we *might* have some time to recover, but Monday's list is already looming. In the midst of it all we think, "This isn't what I had planned. Do other people live this way? Why do they all seem so happy?" Then we hear the car behind us honking as we look up into the green light and zoom off in yet another direction.

Where does it all come from? Did someone generate the long list of items in the daily grind as necessary for a happy life? And when did we subscribe for the regular updates to the never-ending list? The items on the list change somewhat over time, but the *fact* of the list's *existence* does not. We think that once the items on the list are checked off we can finally get down to enjoying life for real. Then it will all be okay. But that day never seems to arrive. The farther we go, the more distant happiness seems, hiding behind the next hill to climb, obstacle to surmount, or dilemma to resolve.

The problem is not *that* we are busy or occupied with daily tasks and responsibilities. This comes with being a mature adult. What *blocks us* is the *way* we are busy and occupied with them. The routine errands, tasks, and intense moments that make up our life all get hijacked from their true purpose to somehow be a barometer we constantly check to gauge our self-worth. And the pressure always seems to rise. Yes, busyness and activity are somewhat natural. The *way* so many of us choose to be busy is not. As we rush around, we tolerate no room for weakness, unevenness, or even ordinariness. We want banner returns and high payouts. We bribe reality and day-to-day life. Rather than exercising reliable and dependable accountability, we are often compulsively busy and extremely preoccupied. We do not live from the *inside out*; we live from the *outside in*. We subtly turn everything around us into some kind of payoff.

It is one thing to be a busy person but quite another to be compulsively so. As we accomplish our tasks, we often still feel *empty*. It is as if the difficult, complicated moments of life's last hours, days, or weeks, and the carefree times of celebration and joy evaporate as soon as they begin. This is because while we may accomplish our daily tasks, the high energy compulsively driving us thrives unsated, ready to latch onto the next tasks as they pile up. When we finally do find time for God, we enlist him as well.

The compulsive lifestyle not only weighs down on and empties our everyday life, but it also squeezes out God. The only way to fit God in to our hectic pace is to attempt to shrink him down and compartmentalize him. We often smuggle our daily compulsivity and worry into our relationship with God, and these take over our prayer and practice of the faith. Worn down, we are tempted to give up on prayer and faith practice and just go through the motions. But we can never shrink down God. God is not a "LandLord." He does not just sit on the sidelines waiting for the bill to come due.

Mercifully, God is not merely a galactic manager or our celestial executive assistant. God is much more. Infinitely more. God is love (see 1 Jn 4:8). God *loves* us, so he *waits*.

He *waits* as we grasp onto our conception of him and try to fit him into our beliefs about the world and life. Isn't it odd? We are supposed to believe in God, but so many of us interpret that *in reverse*: We want God to fit into our beliefs. Essentially we want God *to believe in us*. It is not as sinister as it sounds: *We want to believe in him*, but we *interpret that primarily as him believing in us*. That is our modern default. It is not out-and-out atheism. It is just getting things backward. It seems almost rational: we learned, somewhere in the past, that God loves us and wants to help us, didn't we? So why would we not want to *help him* help us? Since we know our lives so well, why not just point out to God all the things he could do to help us? It would save him work and save us time. After all, he could snap his fingers and make us look just like the people we see in the advertisements. So let's bring him the whole list of things. Let's make our list *his* list. And we start to *expect* things from God. This is when we turn him into the Land-Lord. But God refuses to be anything other than who he is, because he is love and loves us. Pope Benedict XVI reaffirms that the encounter with God's immeasurable divine love transforms us.[3] The Holy Father emphasizes that the word of God is not far from us; his word can enter at any moment into dialogue with our everyday difficulties and problems.[4]

In a technological world of immediate gratification we forget that *humbly asking* God for something and *expecting something* from God are two very different things. Expectations can quickly become requirements we insist on. If our prayer fills up with expectations, and those expectations are not met in the manner we anticipate, we may be tempted to give up on prayer. But expectations have little to do with prayer. In fact, mercy, not expectations, is the soul of prayer.[5] Could it be that the expectations we have *of God* are the biggest things that get in the way between us *and God*? Our expectations of God do not weigh *him* down; they weigh *us* down. They hold *us* back. They lead *us* to bypass God. With our expectations, we fall into the temptation to make our faith life something complicated and compulsive. We mistake the energy around this compulsivity for "progress" or "zeal." As with many areas of our daily life, we set up hoops to jump through to make ourselves feel okay. And when we grow tired of jumping we expect God to jump. But God doesn't jump. *God waits*. And, the God

---

3. See Pope Benedict XVI, *Verbum Domini*, 50.

4. See ibid., 23.

5. See Prosper Grech, *An Outline of New Testament Spirituality*, 43.

of mercy, ever faithful, loyal, and kind, *waits with excitement.* He knows that devotion and the grace-filled act of faith are much deeper and take us to places we would have never imagined. He waits for us to leave the hoops behind.

God's fidelity is not built on our getting what we want; nor is our own fidelity. In fact, fidelity often has more to do with us *not getting* everything we want. This is why we cling to God's promise even in dark times. The act of faith that we make in Baptism and reaffirm throughout our life in the sacraments engages mysteries far deeper than we often know. While we are busy with expectations, God is busy with mystery. Adrienne von Speyr notes that God's mysteries hide everywhere.[6]

Many of us at some point feel or believe we can only approach God or pray once we "feel okay" inside, once we "fix" our complicated lives. This belief is a mistake. *God waits.* He wants us to bring our rough edges to him now, today, in this moment. He wants us to bring our worries, wounds, busyness, and burdens to him.

Listening is in God's very nature. God hears listening best of all. Even a prayer of asking, what we call a prayer of petition, must take the form of listening for God. Then he hears us, and we hear him. And in hearing him we are *led* to all we need or desire.

The purpose of this book is for it to get out of the way. Only now can this book's true purpose be fulfilled: for it to be put down by the reader so that the reader can entrust his or her life ever more fully and completely to the word of God. The Holy Spirit has laid the foundation for this trust deep in our hearts. Hopefully, the previous pages have helped to uncover the Spirit's

---

6. See Adrienne von Speyr, *The Letter to the Colossians,* 136.

groundwork and open a new path. Someone is waiting for us on the path—our Blessed Mother Mary. She knows its ways so well, is familiar with its twists and turns, its ups and downs. As we put this book down, she takes our hand and whispers, "Do whatever he tells you" (Jn 2:5).

Select Bibliography

Ambrose. "The Prayer of Job and David." Trans. Michael P. McHugh, *Seven Exegetical Works of Fathers of the Church: A New Translation*, vol. 65. Washington, DC: The Catholic University of America Press, 1972.

Aquinas, Thomas. *Summa Theologiae*. In *Basic Writings of Saint Thomas Aquinas*. Ed. Anton C. Pegis. New York: Random House, 1945.

Augustine. *City of God*.

———. *Letters, 3 (131–164)*. Trans. Sister Wilfrid Parsons, SND, *Fathers of the Church: A New Translation*, vol. 20. Washington, DC: The Catholic University of America Press, 1953.

———. "Tractates on the Gospel of John 1–10." Trans. John W. Rettig, *Fathers of the Church: A New Translation*, vol. 78. Washington, DC: The Catholic University of America Press, 1947.

———. *On the Psalms*. Ed. Philip Schaff. *Nicene and Post Nicene Fathers*, vol. 8. Peabody, MA: Hendrickson Publishers, 2004.

———. *The Works of Saint Augustine: A Translation for the Twenty-First Century*, vol. III/5. Edited by John E. Rotelle. New York: New City Press, 1992.

Balthasar, Hans Urs von. *Christian Meditation*. San Francisco: Ignatius Press, 1989.

———. *Explorations in Theology I: The Word Made Flesh*. San Francisco: Ignatius Press, 1989.

————. *The Glory of the Lord: A Theological Aesthetics I: Seeing the Form.* San Francisco: Ignatius Press, 1989.

————. *The Glory of the Lord: A Theological Aesthetics VII: Theology: The New Covenant.* San Francisco: Ignatius Press, 1989.

————. *Mysterium Paschale.* Grand Rapids, MI: Wm. B. Eerdmans Publishing Company, 1990.

————. *Theo-Drama IV: The Action.* San Francisco: Ignatius Press, 1994.

————. *Theo-Drama V: The Last Act.* San Francisco: Ignatius Press, 1994.

————. *Theo-Logic III: The Spirit of Truth.* San Francisco: Ignatius Press, 2005.

————. *Unless You Become Like This Child.* San Francisco: Ignatius Press, 1991.

Bede the Venerable. *Homilies on the Gospels Book Two: Lent to the Dedication of the Church.* Trans. Lawrence T. Martin and David Hurst. Kalamazoo, MI: Cistercian Publications, 1991.

Bernanos, Georges. "Sermon of an Agnostic on the Feast of Saint Thérèse." In *The Heroic Face of Innocence: Three Stories by Georges Bernanos.* Grand Rapids, MI: Wm. B. Eerdmans Publishing Company, 1999.

Bernard of Clairvaux. *Homilies in Praise of the Virgin Mother.* Kalamazoo, MI: Cistercian Publications, 1993.

————. "Homily for the Fourth Sunday After Pentecost." In *Sermons for the Summer Season: Liturgical Sermons from Rogationtide to Pentecost.* Kalamazoo, MI: Cistercian Publications, 1990.

Bonaventure. *Commentary on the Gospel of Luke.* Ed. Robert J. Karris, OFM, *Works of Saint Bonaventure, Volume VIII, Part I.* Saint Bonaventure, NY: Franciscan Institute Publications.

Caesarius of Arles. *Sermons, Volume II (81–186).* Trans. Mary Magdeleine Mueller, *Fathers of the Church: A New Translation,* vol. 47. Washington DC: The Catholic University of America Press, 1947.

Cyril of Alexandria, *Commentary on Luke*. Trans. R. Payne Smith. New York: Studion Publishers, 1983.

Daniélou, Jean. *The Infancy Narratives*. New York: Herder and Herder, 1968.

———. *The Work of John the Baptist*. Baltimore: Helicon Press, Inc., 1966.

Davies, Oliver. *A Theology of Compassion: Metaphysics of Difference and the Renewal of Tradition*. Grand Rapids, MI: Wm. B. Eerdmans Publishing Company, 2001.

De la Potterie, Ignace. *The Hour of Jesus: The Passion and the Resurrection of Jesus According to John*. New York: Alba House, 1989.

De Lubac, Henri. *Scripture in the Tradition*. New York: Herder and Herder, 2001.

De Margerie, Bertrand, SJ. *The Christian Trinity in History: Studies in Historical Theology*. Massachusetts: Saint Bede's Press, 1982.

German Bishops' Conference. *The Church's Confession of Faith: A Catholic Catechism for Adults*. San Francisco: Ignatius Press Communio Books, 1987.

Gillette, Gertrude, OSB. *Four Faces of Anger: Seneca, Evagrius Ponticus, Cassian, and Augustine*. Lanham, MD: University Press of America, 2010.

Grech, Prosper. *An Outline of New Testament Spirituality*. Grand Rapids, MI: Wm. B. Eerdmans Publishing Company, 2011.

———. *Acts of the Apostles Explained: A Doctrinal Commentary*. New York: Alba House, 1966.

Gregory the Great, "Homily 34, Sections 7 and 9." In *Forty Gospel Homilies.* Piscataway, NJ: Gorgias Press, 2009.

———. *Moralia in Job*, vol. 1. Trans. J. H. Parker, *A Library of Fathers of the Holy Catholic Church*. Oxford: J. H. Parker 1844–1850.

Guerric of Igny, *Liturgical Sermons Book 2*. Kalamazoo, MI: Cistercian Publications, 1971.

Hugh of Balma. "The Roads to Zion Mourn." Trans. Dennis Martin, *Carthusian Spirituality: The Writings of Hugh of Balma and Guigo de Ponte,* The Classics of Western Spirituality Series. Mahwah, NJ: Paulist Press, 1997.

Humbert of Romans. "Treatise on the Formation of Preachers." Ed. Simon Tugwell. *Early Dominicans: Selected Writings,* The Classics of Western Spirituality Series. Mahwah, NJ: Paulist Press, 1982.

International Theological Commission. *Theology Today: Perspectives, Principles and Criteria.* Rome: Libreria Editrice Vaticana, 2012.

Jerome. *Homilies on the Psalms (1–59).* Trans. Marie Liguori Ewald, IHM, *Fathers of the Church: A New Translation,* vol. 48. Washington DC: The Catholic University of America Press, 1964.

Journet, Charles. *What Is Dogma?* San Francisco: Ignatius Press, 2011.

Laffitte, Jean. "Love and Forgiveness." Ed. Livio Melina and Carl Anderson. *The Way of Love: Reflections on Pope Benedict XVI's Encyclical "Deus Caritas Est."* San Francisco: Ignatius Press, 2006.

Leiva-Merikakis, Erasmo. *Fire of Mercy, Heart of the Word: Meditations on the Gospel According to Saint Matthew,* vol. 1. San Francisco: Ignatius Press, 1996.

Leo I. *Sermons.* Trans. Jane Patricia Freeland. *Fathers of the Church: A New Translation,* vol. 93. Washington, DC: The Catholic University of America Press, 1996.

Leo I. Leo the Great. Ed. P. Schaff, et al. *A Select Library of the Nicene and Post-Nicene Fathers of the Christian Church.* Grand Rapids, MI: Eerdmans Press, 1969.

Léon-Dufour, Xavier. *Resurrection and the Message of Easter.* New York: Holt, Rinehart, and Winston, 1975.

Liguori, Saint Alphonsus. "Conversing with God as a Friend." Ed. Frederick M. Jones. *Alphonsus de Liguori: Selected Writings.* The Classics of Western Spirituality Series. Mahwah, NJ: Paulist Press, 1999.

Martimort, A. G., et al., "The Liturgy and Time." In *The Church at Prayer*, vol. IV. Collegeville, MN: The Liturgical Press, 1986.

Martin, Linette. *Practical Praying*. Grand Rapids, MI: Eerdmans Press, 1997.

McNabb, Vincent, OP. *The Craft of Prayer*. London: Burns, Oates and Washbourne, 1935.

Melina, Livio. *Building a Culture of the Family: The Language of Love*. Staten Island, NY: Alba House, 2011.

More, Thomas. *The Sadness of Christ*. New Rochelle, NY: Scepter Press, 1993.

Murray, Paul, OP. *The New Wine of Dominican Spirituality: A Drink Called Happiness*. London: Burns and Oates, 2011.

————. *A Journey with Jonah: The Spirituality of Bewilderment*. Dublin: The Columba Press, 2002.

Nicolas of Strasbourg. *The Sermon on the Golden Mountain* in *Late Medieval Mysticism of the Low Countries*. Ed. Rik van Nieuwenhove, et. al. The Classics of Western Spirituality Series. Mahwah, NJ: Paulist Press, 2008.

Origen, *Homilies on Luke*. Trans. Joseph T. Lienhard. *Fathers of the Church: A New Translation*, vol. 94. Washington, DC: The Catholic University of America Press, 2009.

Pinckaers, Servais, OP. *Morality: The Catholic View*. South Bend, IN: Saint Augustine's Press, 2001.

Pinckaers, Servais, OP. *The Sources of Christian Ethics*. Washington, DC: The Catholic University of America Press, 1995.

Pollard, Miriam, OCSO. "Holy Saturday." In *Neither Be Afraid and Other Poems*. San Francisco: Ignatius Press, 2000.

Rigali, Cardinal Justin. *Red Mass Homily*, October 5, 2009, http://archphila.org/rigali/cardhom/redmassscranton.htm.

Sarna, Nahum M., gen. ed. and commentary. *Genesis: The JPS Torah Commentary*. Philadelphia: The Jewish Publication Society, 1989.

Savage, Anne, and Nicholas Watson, trans. *Anchoritic Spirituality: Ancrene Wisse and Associated Works*. The Classics of Western Spirituality Series. Mahwah, NJ: Paulist Press, 1991.

Saward, John. *Cradle of Redeeming Love: The Theology of the Christmas Mystery*. San Francisco: Ignatius Press, 2002.

————. *Redeemer in the Womb*. San Francisco: Ignatius Press, 1993.

————. *The Way of the Lamb: The Spirit of Childhood and the End of the Age*. San Francisco: Ignatius Press, 1999.

Tauler, Johannes. *Sermons*, Trans. Maria Shrady. The Classics of Western Spirituality Series. Mahwah, NJ: Paulist Press, 1985.

Teresa of Avila. *The Interior Castle*. Trans. Otilio Rodriguez, OCD, and Kieran Kavanaugh, OCD, *The Collected Works of Saint Teresa of Avila*. Washington DC: ICS Publications, 1980.

The Assessment of Inner Stirrings. Trans. James Walsh, SJ, *The Pursuit of Wisdom and Other Works by the Author of the Cloud of Unknowing*. The Classics of Western Spirituality Series. Mahwah, NJ: Paulist Press, 1988.

The Cloud of Unknowing. Trans. James Walsh, SJ. The Classics of Western Spirituality Series. Mahwah, NJ: Paulist Press, 1981.

Teresa Benedicta of the Cross. *The Science of the Cross*. Washington, DC: ICS Publications, 2002.

Torrell, Jean-Pierre, OP. *Christ and Spirituality in Saint Thomas Aquinas*. Washington, DC: The Catholic University of America Press, 2011.

————. *Thomas Aquinas*, vol. 2, *Spiritual Master*. Washington, DC: The Catholic University of America Press, 2003.

Tugwell, Simon, OP. *Prayer: Living With God*. Springfield, IL: Templegate, 1975.

————. *The Beatitudes: Soundings in Christian Tradition*. London: Darton, Longman, and Todd, Ltd., 1985.

Von Speyr, Adrienne. *Job*. Freiburg, Germany: Johannes Verlag Einsiedeln, 1972.

————. *John: The Discourses of Controversy.* San Francisco: Ignatius Press, 1993.

————. *Mark: Meditations on the Gospel of Mark.* San Francisco: Ignatius Press, 2012.

————. *The Letter to the Colossians.* San Francisco: Ignatius Press, 1998.

————. *The Letter to the Ephesians.* San Francisco: Ignatius Press, 1996.

————. *The World of Prayer.* San Francisco: Ignatius Press, 1985.

Magisterial Documents

Benedict XVI. *Dogma and Preaching: Applying Christian Doctrine to Daily Life,* First unabridged edition. San Francisco: Ignatius Press, 2011.

————. *Jesus of Nazareth: From the Baptism in the Jordan to the Transfiguration.* New York: Doubleday, 2007.

————. *Jesus of Nazareth: Holy Week: From the Entrance into Jerusalem to the Resurrection.* San Francisco: Ignatius Press, 2011.

————. *Spe Salvi.* Boston: Pauline Books & Media, 2007.

————. *Verbum Domini.* Boston: Pauline Books & Media, 2010.

Catechism of the Catholic Church, Second edition. Washington, DC: United States Conference of Catholic Bishops, 2006.

Congregation for the Doctrine of the Faith. Letter to the Bishops of the Catholic Church on Some Aspects of Christian Meditation, 1989.

John Paul II. *Dominum et Vivificantem.* Boston: Pauline Books & Media, 1986.

————. *Evangelium Vitae.* Boston: Pauline Books & Media, 1995.

————. *God, Father and Creator: A Catechesis on the Creed.* Boston: Pauline Books & Media, 1996.

————. *Jesus, Son and Savior: A Catechesis on the Creed*, vol. II. Boston: Pauline Books & Media, 1996.

————. *Man and Woman He Created Them: A Theology of the Body*. Boston: Pauline Books & Media, 2006.

————. *The Spirit Giver of Life and Love: A Catechesis on the Creed, Volume III*. Boston: Pauline Books & Media, 1996.

————. *Veritatis Splendor*. Boston: Pauline Books & Media, 1993.

Pontifical Biblical Commission. *The Bible and Morality: Biblical Roots of Christian Conduct*. Rome: Libreria Editrice Vaticana, 2008.

Vatican Council II. *Gaudium et Spes*. Boston: Pauline Books & Media, 1965.

Vatican Council II. *Sacrosanctum Concilium*. Boston: Pauline Books & Media, 1964.

Credits